TRANSPORT FOR
THE SPACE ECONOMY

Transport for the Space Economy
a geographical study

ALAN HAY

Department of Geography, University of Sheffield

University of Washington Press
Seattle

© Alan M. Hay 1973

Published by the University of Washington Press, 1973
Printed in Great Britain

Library of Congress Cataloging in Publication Data

Hay, Alan M
 Transport for the space economy.

 Includes bibliographical references.
 1. Transportation. I. Title.
HE151.H33   380.5   73–10604
ISBN   0–295–95306–3

For A.M.H., E.E.H. and P.A.H.

Contents

vii

List of Figures

List of Tables

Preface

This book attempts to bring order to a diverse field, and in so doing to fill a gap of which I have been aware as student, research worker and teacher. Although the book draws its inspiration from geography —particularly the recent literature on locational analysis—this limits neither the literature surveyed nor I hope the range of people who will find the discussion of value. With a wider readership in mind I have attempted to write in such a fashion that even those who have little geographical or statistical training will be able to grasp the main arguments, but some introductory reading for them is listed at the beginning of the bibliographical notes.

In writing I have been constantly reminded of the debt I owe to teachers, colleagues and students. Among the first, three should be mentioned by name: Mr F. G. Self of Norwich School, Mr A. A. L. Caesar of St Catharine's College, Cambridge, and Professor Peter Haggett, then of Cambridge and now of Bristol. Each one of them has taught me much; this book is a poor reflection of the standards which they set. Among those I count as colleagues I would like to mention three also: Bob Smith whose help on many topics has clarified my thinking, my brother Donald who has always been a trenchant critic of my ideas, and Michael Chisholm who, as the publisher's adviser, persuaded me to write, to keep on writing and to improve my early drafts. Many other colleagues at Ibadan, Leicester, Madison and Sheffield have helped me, as have many unknown to me personally but whose work I have quoted in the following pages: if this is too brief an acknowledgement I ask their forgiveness. My students at Leicester listened to early versions of this book; their views, their questions, their incomprehension and even their examination scripts have all contributed to this final version. None of these people bears any responsibility for my errors and omissions.

Drafts of the book were typed by Jean Smith and Monica Long. I am grateful to both these people.

I would like to acknowledge the advice of Professor Ullman of the

University of Washington and Dr Fullerton of the University of
Newcastle upon Tyne, both of whom read the final draft and made
valuable suggestions.

Finally I owe a debt to the members of my family: and to three of
them this book is dedicated.

ALAN HAY

Sheffield, 1973

1 Introduction

Transport studies have great practical importance, and it is the desire to solve problems of transport investment, operations and regulation which has stimulated a rapid growth in transport studies. This policy orientation has tended to obscure the development of systematic investigations within such disciplines as economics, engineering and geography. The aim of this study is to provide a systematic framework for the description, analysis and explanation of the spatial patterns in transport phenomena. Such a framework must inevitably use the findings of many disciplines even though the conceptual organisation is geographical in derivation.

A Framework for Study

The framework followed in this study is presented in figure 1.1. Four major topics are identified which together form the central sections of this book. The *demand* for transportation is seen as the fundamental basis of explanation. The supply of both *network facilities* and *vehicle capacity* is seen as a response to demand. Both these topics are defined in their widest sense: networks to include both routeway and terminal facilities, vehicle capacity to cover all forms of carrying capacity including shipping and aircraft. Demand, networks and vehicle supply are seen as the determinants of the spatial pattern of transport *flows*. The relations between these phenomena include much circular causation, but some major casual links are suggested in the diagram.

The framework also recognises two types of peripheral topic. Firstly, there are some topics which though non-spatial are essential for understanding the overall spatial patterns; *vice versa* there are some topics which though spatial contribute little to the central analysis. These two groups are identified as *convergent non-spatial* and *divergent spatial* topics in figure 1.1.

An important consequence of the framework is the balance of the book. Some topics have attracted much attention from other writers, either because of their pragmatic importance or because of

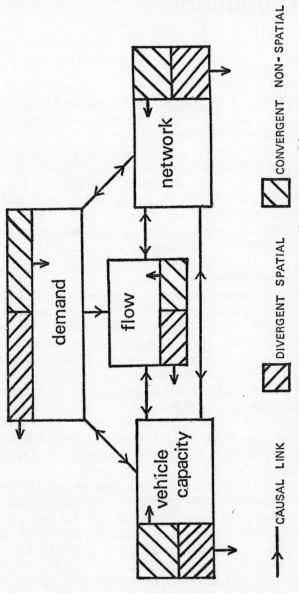

Fig. 1.1. Elements in the spatial analysis of transport problems

CAUSAL LINK

DIVERGENT SPATIAL

CONVERGENT NON-SPATIAL

their importance in the framework of other disciplines. In contrast, there are other topics, integral to this framework, which are almost neglected in the literature. This book seeks to reflect the balance of the framework and not that of the published literature.

The Relation of the Framework to Geographical Studies of Transport

The study of transport geography is a lively aspect of the discipline. Its liveliness is evident in both the number of its practitioners and the quality of their published work. Despite this the topic is neglected by many standard works on geography as a whole: for example the important study of geographical methodology by Hartshorne barely acknowledges the existence of transport geography.[1] It is therefore necessary to identify the origins of the subject and the main categories of work which its proponents have undertaken. A useful starting point for such discussion is the work of Hettner, especially the paper published by him in 1897, under the title 'Der gegenwartige Stand der Verkehrsgeographie'.[2] This paper is important in its own right for two reasons. Firstly, it was a systematic discussion of *Verkehrsgeographie* as a topic of research in which the final objective is an understanding of flow systems. Secondly, Hettner related this to a general methodology of the subject based upon 'areal differentiation'. The paper is also important for a third reason. Hettner expounded his concepts with a reference to the circulation of the bloodstream.[3] There is strong evidence that this analogy was the origin of a French concept, *géographie de la circulation*. The reasons for this supposition are threefold: the presence of the analogy, the explicit reference to Hettner by Huckel, who seems to have introduced *circulation* into French geography,[4] and finally the fact that German–French dictionaries of the period offer *circulation* as a translation of *Verkehr*.[5] In Huckel and other French writers the concept of *circulation* has been extended to cover all movement systems,[6] an approach which has been severely criticised on the grounds that unlike systems are treated on a common basis. A clear expression of this criticism is given by Vasilievskiy: 'the geography of transportation is part of the . . . geography of material production . . . . the so-called *géographie de circulation* of the French is erroneous'.[7]

The principal objectives of the Hettner–Huckel approach have, however, been reaffirmed at various times. For example, Crowe wrote: 'In thus turning to transport as the effective regionalising principle ... stress is to be laid not upon terminal facilities, not on the pattern of the system, but upon men and things moving'[8]. A similar view has been taken by Ullman in the postwar period,[9] and it is to this tradition that the present work looks for inspiration.

There are, however, two other traditions in the subject which deserve mention. The 'morphological' tradition is concerned almost exclusively with visible landscape forms, the networks, the routes and the terminals. This tradition has been widely accepted in England and is ably defended by Appleton.[10] It has also, despite lip service to *circulation*, become a dominant theme in French writing.[11] A second tradition is concerned with the impact of transport upon the geography of areas. It is explicitly recognised by Sorre[12] and has been widely adopted in Britain[13] and the United States.[14] Part, at least, of this attention has been policy orientated, and has not claimed any justification in terms of the discipline.

The Framework in relation to Transport Economics

The alleged failure of economics to deal adequately with geographic space has been examined in many recent studies. Chisholm, for example, quotes Marshall: 'this element of time requires more careful attention just now than does that of space'.[15] This a-spatial character of much economic analysis has been reflected in transport economies because, as Munby noted, 'there is no special economics of transport, but only general economic theory applied to transport problems'.[16] For this reason studies in the economics of transport have been concerned with classical problems of demand, supply, price, competition and monopoly, often without explicit recognition of their spatial attributes.[17]

A central problem has been the identification of the utility of transport. As early as 1844 Dupuit argued that the utility of transport (in other words, change of location) is measurable only for specified amounts of a commodity supplied to a specified consumer.[18] This problem is further complicated by the fact that all, or nearly all, transport demands are derived from the demand for some other good such as food, shelter or recreation. A second field of transport economics has been the study of costs. The relation between the main categories of cost are particularly complex in transport economics; indeed some authorities suggest that the classical distinctions are inapplicable in this field. In addition to the problem of accounting for such recognised costs, there are many 'hidden costs' of inherited facilities and of social diseconomies. The search for real costs has therefore been a major topic of inquiry. Linking both utility and cost problems is the question of pricing under both competition and monopoly conditions. The principles of rate-making, and the results of their application, have likewise attracted much attention. Included in these analyses has been a recognition of the spatial implications of terminal charges and of rate tapers.

All three topics have impinged upon the application of transport economics to decision making. The first application was to the regulation of individual transport industries to prevent 'excessive competition'. This analysis was applied to railways in the nineteenth century and to road transport from the 1920s, and in recent years has been extended to air transport operation. It was only a short step from such policy to the regulation of relations between transport industries. Here economists found themselves defining the correct roles of the transport media and suggesting appropriate measures to achieve the desired pattern. Finally, it has been recognised that wise transport investment is dependent upon accurate traffic forecasts, and these have therefore engaged the attention of transport economists.

The relevance of the present framework to practical problems of transport economics and policy is not immediately evident, but it is an assumption of this study that precise description, rigorous analysis and coherent explanation are a prerequisite of decision making. Thus no attempt is made to treat practical problems as such in the central part of the text. The final chapter, however, outlines the problems of planning for transport and identifies the relevance of some spatial analytical tools in their solution.

2 Transport Demand

The geography of transport demand is neglected by many scholars. It is, for example, excluded by Smith from the threefold aims of transport geography which he identifies.[1] It finds no mention in Appleton's methodological paper,[2] and it is almost absent from the methodology sketched in standard texts.[3] Perle, it is true, offers a study of the demand for transportation, but he focuses almost entirely upon the price elasticities of demand, chiefly as they determine the sharing of traffic between road and rail transport.[4] Yet the systematic study of demand is important for two reasons. Firstly, without a prior understanding of demand any explanation of routes and flows will necessarily be incomplete. Secondly, it is the study of transport demand which links geography most clearly to the rest of geography. The patterns of production and consumption, population, residence and employment are the classical topics of geographic investigation; they are also the fundamental raw material for an investigation of transport demand.

2.1 THE ELEMENTS OF TRANSPORT DEMAND

An intuitive appraisal of transport demand identifies three elements: origins, destinations and volumes. A cartographic analysis of these elements can be achieved using quite simple techniques, including proportional symbols, divided proportional symbols[5] and desire lines[6] (figure 2.1). Although these techniques can be effective diagnostic tools they suffer, in common with most cartographic approaches, from two flaws. Firstly, the impact is entirely visual, and even this impact is lost when complex situations are portrayed. Secondly, the map is an end in itself and thus ill suited to further analysis.

The origin–destination table or matrix is a more powerful device (table 2.1). It reveals more elements of the nature of transport demand, it is capable of extension into further methods of analysis, and it is well suited for electronic data processing; it is thus useful even where

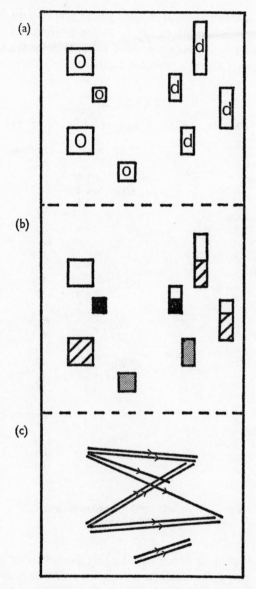

Fig. 2.1. Elementary maps of transport demand

the problems are complex or the amounts of data very large. Consider an origin–destination matrix (*a*). In such a matrix the locations are specified as rows and columns. Row totals indicate the total traffic originating at a location; column totals similarly indicate the total

TABLE 2.1

THE MATRIX PRESENTATION OF TRANSPORT DEMAND

			Destinations		
			A	B	
(*a*)	*Locations*				
	(tonnes)	1			20
	Origins:	2			30
		3			40
			35	55	90

			Destinations		
			A	B	
(*b*)	*Distances*				
	(kilometres)	1	30	15	
	Origins:	2	20	10	
		3	10	25	

			Destinations		
			A	B	
(*c*)	*Flows*				
	(tonnes)	1	5	15	20
	Origins:	2	15	15	30
		3	15	25	40
			35	55	90

			Destinations		
			A	B	
(*d*)	*Output*				
	(tonne-kilometres)	1	150	225	375
	Origins:	2	300	150	450
		3	150	625	775
			600	1000	1600

Total output demanded: 1600 tonne-kilometres
Average length of haul: 17·8 kilometres

traffic terminating at a location. An origin–destination matrix with only these row and column totals known is the most fundamental specification of a transport demand in geographic terms. The degree of spatial separation of the origins and destinations can be recorded in a second matrix of distances (*b*). If these are geodetic distances, demand is expressed in its most abstract form: alternatively the rather greater route distances will express the demand in more realistic terms. The two matrices together specify the basic demand for transport and are thus equivalent to figure 2.1a.

The insertion of cell values in the matrix is equivalent to specifying the flow volumes between locations and is therefore also equivalent to figure 2.1b and c. This makes it possible to determine the output demanded from the transport system. Multiplication of the corresponding cells in the volume matrix (*c*) and the distance matrix (*b*) yields an output matrix (*d*) in which the units are of output (work done equals distance × volume, for example ton-miles or passenger-kilometres). Division of the aggregate output by aggregate volume yields another common statistic, the mean length of haul or mean trip length.

It can be observed that although the matrices *a* and *b* indicate the geographic basis of demand they do not specify the output demanded or the mean length of haul. Only if the pattern of flows is specified (that is, if the cell values are specified, as in matrix *c*) is total demand determined. On the other hand the matrices *a* and *b* for a homogeneous commodity do specify the minimum demand for transport which would arise if the most efficient pattern of flows could be specified. The available procedures for identifying such an efficient system, in terms of outputs or costs subject to such factors as constraints on capacity, will be examined in a later chapter.[7] The raw material for such analyses is provided by matrices of the forms *a* and *b*.

Spatial Types of Demand

Examination of maps or matrices reveals that demands differ in their spatial characteristics. Four main types of pattern can be distinguished. In some areas the demand is essentially a matter of *distribution* from a few origins to a number of spatially dispersed destinations. It is common in the demand by manufacturing industry for the transport of the finished product. Secondly, there are *collection* systems in which the number of destinations is smaller than a large number of origins dispersed in geographic space. It occurs, for example, in nearly all agricultural systems. The other two spatial types are less common. *Point to point* patterns occur in the movement of inter-mediate goods between manufacturing plants and may also occur in the supply of minerals and fuels to industrial plants. *Area to area* demands rarely occur in freight transport but are important for many passenger demands within cities.

Although such a typology is conceptually valid, its application is dependent upon both the scale of analysis and the organisation of commodity movement. The geographical scale of analysis will determine whether a producing or consuming activity may be legitimately considered as a point or as an area. In an interregional trade study, for example, a city may be considered as a point, but in intra-urban studies it can be considered as an areally dispersed transport demand. The organisation of movement may similarly transform the spatial pattern of a demand. The role of wholesaling functions in commodity trades is, at least in part, to transform a point to area demand into a sequence of point to point, and point to area.

The Density and Dispersion of Demand

It is frequently useful to be able to express the demand for transport arising at a point or within an area. It will be clear that most demands cannot be conceived as arising at a single point—although this is in part a function of scale of analysis—and it is therefore necessary to measure demand density within an area, or the degree of dispersion of demand around some stated point.

The density of demand per unit area may be expressed in volume per unit area (passengers per square mile or tonnages per square kilometre) or in output terms (passenger-miles per square mile or ton kilometres per square kilometre). Although the first density measure is likely to show wide variations in geographic space, much location theory would imply that output demand for transport will be much less variable. Consider for example the demand for transport within a city. The classic theories of urban form imply that, as distance from the city centre increases, the density of persons requiring transport to the centre falls. Similarly the von Thunen type analyses of agricultural location imply that, as distance from the market centre increases, so the tonnage of products requiring transport to that centre will fall.

The dispersion of demand within an area is best measured as mean distance or the standard distance deviation from the mean centre of the distribution. These measures are fully discussed by such authors as Timms[8] and Neft.[9] The mean distance has a direct interpretation in transport terms as the length of haul which would be involved in assembling demand at a single point. Alternatively the distances may be calculated from some arbitrary point within the area such as an established or proposed transport terminal. In all cases the calculations must be weighted according to volume.

Problems of Empirical Investigation

Any empirical investigation of transport demand encounters severe data problems. In some cases the full pattern of supply from producing locations to consuming locations is known, but in many cases, accounting for a large proportion of aggregate transport demand, the data are not available.

In some cases there are accurate data on the distribution of complementary economic or social activities but none on the movement pattern by which these locations are matched. For example census data may record the number of employed persons in residential areas, similar inquiries may record the distribution of employment, but there may be no information about flows from residential areas to employment locations. In matrix terms the row and column totals are known but not the cell values. In such a case it may be necessary to carry out sample surveys to establish the estimated flows between locations. This type of problem is recurrent in town planning studies.[10]

The study of the demand for interregional transport in complex economies is even more difficult to assess. Although the geographical distribution of production is usually recorded in some form, there is seldom any estimate of the regional distribution of consumption or of the flow patterns which exist within the system. It is only rarely possible to collect data on a large enough scale to eliminate this lack of information. In other cases it is necessary to estimate the pattern of consumption from known regional populations and national averages on consumption.[11] Similarly, if interregional input–output tables can be constructed, they imply a demand for transport by sectors and in aggregate; but independent monitoring of interregional flows is often a prerequisite for the construction of such tables.[12] More sophisticated studies may weight the estimate according to known data on incomes, demographic structure, and so on. The final estimates of transport demand volumes and locations must then be used to estimate the directions, distances, output and trip length which the system is likely to assume. Planning studies have adapted explanatory theories of flow in order to predict these characteristics.[13] The results of such predictions can be used for planning and may be used in the study of demand for network capacity; unless circular argument is admitted, they cannot be used as independent variables in the study of flow systems.

Finally, empirical investigation will reveal the instability of spatial patterns of transport demand. They are responsive to changes in the costs of transport and the structure of the transport network, and they also change as a result of entirely extraneous processes, so that they show rapid changes over time.

2.2 THE ECONOMIC NATURE OF TRANSPORT DEMAND

Demand for transport is not a fundamental human need, unlike the need for food, clothing, warmth and shelter. It is usually derived from the demand for 'the necessities of life', and direct demand (movement for movement's sake) is comparatively rare.[14] Not only is demand largely derived but much of it is not explicitly recognised by the individuals concerned. For example most individuals will recognise their demand for transport to a place of employment, but will not realise that their normal pattern of household consumption implies an equally important demand for the transport of commodities. In a developed economy and society this unrecognised demand is expressed by intermediaries such as food wholesalers, who also pass on the cost of transport in the prices of goods and services. An increase in transport costs will be reflected in the price of goods and services, and the demand for transport will be indirectly affected by changes in the demand for those goods and services. Such changes may occur in three ways: changes in the output and trip length of demand (though locations and volumes are unchanged), changes in the volume of demand (though locations are unchanged) and changes in the location of demand itself.

The Response of Demand to Cost: Output and Trip Length

The interdependence of transport costs and transport demand can be illustrated in two ways. An *a priori* argument, abstracted from reality, can be erected to illustrate principles.[15] Empirical evidence can be used to establish the relevance of such principles even where other factors intervene.

Consider the situation in which a small number of producing

locations produce a constant volume of commodity for consumption at a small number of destinations. It has already been noted that the pattern of flows will usually be sub-optimal, and the output and mean trip length will therefore be greater than minimum because oi inefficiencies in the system. Any increase in the 'real' cost of transport will increase the financial penalty for such inefficiency and may therefore lead to changes in the pattern of flow. Where the system is planned centrally, the results of such changes will be a reduction in output and trip length. If on the other hand the decision making is decentralised, the attempts of each location to optimise its supply pattern may lead to changes in the pattern but not necessarily to a reduction in output or trip length. It is clear that such effects are most likely to be observed in the short term; they are due entirely to changes in the flow pattern with no necessary change in location or volume.

The Effect of Transport Cost on Demand Volumes

It is also possible for changes in the cost of transport to induce changes in the volume of demand where all haul lengths and locations remain constant. Consider an isolated market with an equally isolated supplier, for which the supply and demand curves are known. The volume of goods produced, transported and consumed in the absence of transport costs, according to equilibrium analysis, is determined by the intersection of the demand and supply curves (figure 2.2). If the transport costs are raised by x units, the supply curve can be correspondingly raised to give the supply curve in the consuming region ($S'S'$), a new intersection, and a new and reduced volume produced, transported and traded (V').

A similar effect can be illustrated from the case of two supply locations with identical supply curves at different distances from a market with known demand curve (figure 2.3). In the absence of transport costs the supply curve for the consuming location can be defined as the addition horizontally of the two supply curves; this joint supply (SS) curve intersects with the demand curve to yield an equilibrium volume (V) and price (p). This volume is produced equally at both supply locations and is transported to the market. If transport costs are introduced, the supply curves in the consuming region are raised and the joint supply curve (again by addition) is also raised ($S'S'$) to give a reduced volume to be produced (at price p'), transported

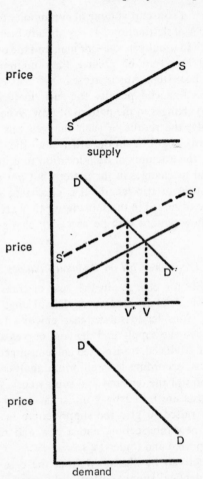

Fig. 2.2. A simple interpretation of interregional transport demand

and consumed. It now becomes clear that because they have different locations the two suppliers have different supply curves in the consuming region, after the introduction of transport costs, and thus will produce different quantities for the market (V_1 and V_2). Thus change in transport costs will in general affect the volume of transport demand by different amounts at different locations, and the effect will be most marked at the locations most remote from the market.

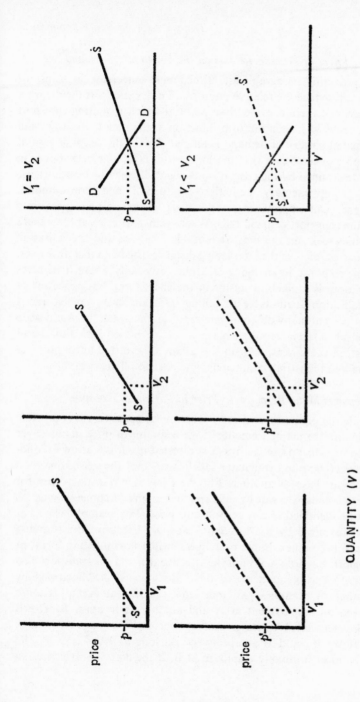

QUANTITY (V)

Fig. 2.3. A simple interpretation of interregional transport demand in a three-region case

The Effect of Transport Costs on the Location of Demand

The preceding paragraph established that a decrease in transport costs will reduce the relative importance of locations. If the diagram is examined there is evidently a point at which mounting transport costs result in a cessation of production at the remote location, and the spatial pattern of demand is altered. This is the simplest case of the more general case that the location of economic activities is in part determined by the costs of movement. If costs of transport are high, complementary activities—production and consumption, residence and employment—tend to be located in close proximity and the transport demand falls. Where transport costs are low these activities seek out the most favourable locations and specialisation ensues regardless of the intervening distances; demand therefore rises.

This response in changing locations, especially where it involves relocation, is unlikely to occur in the short term, but processes of specialisation attributable to falling transport costs can be traced historically at many different geographical scales. On the world scale it is clear in the increasing emergence of specialised agricultural and industrial economies, and on the urban scale in the appearance of specialised industrial, commercial and residential districts.

Elements in the Response to Price in Passenger Transport

Despite the problems outlined in the preceding section it is possible to identify the major elements in the response to price in passenger transport. Most passenger travel is directed towards a known economic objective: employment at a satisfactory level, the sale of one good or the purchase of another. For the passenger transport operator these demands exist side by side, and the varying component demands must be identified in any response to price. For example when bus fares are raised by the London Transport Executive the response to price is complex. Some passengers switch to competing forms of transport, but a reduction in the effective demand for transport also occurs.[16] The components of this reduction can be illustrated by hypothetical examples. An individual resident at A may choose between an employment at A and another at location B. The B employment involves travel costing y pence. The wage rates at A and B are W_a and W_b respectively. As long as $W_b - y > W_a$ he will be most profitably employed at B. If the cost of travel rises so that $W_b - y' < W_a$ there is no profit from the journey and the demand for transport will fall. The argument can be elaborated to illustrate the reverse case, and to include the notional costs of passenger travelling time.

A similar case can be identified of competing sources of supply. A resident at A chooses between retail outlets at A and B. The outlet at B involves travelling at a cost y. The marginal advantages of shopping at B are due to lower price, a greater range of products, and other features attractive to shoppers. It is assumed that these can be quantified as M_a and M_b respectively. As long as $M_b - y > M_a$, shopping continues at B; if the cost of transport rises so that $M_b - y' < M_a$, the demand for transport to B falls.

Personal marketing is rare in the developed world, but is widespread in the developing countries. Farmers, or farmers' wives, accompany produce to market in order to ensure a fair price. (It should be noted that this visit to the market also has a social function, and may therefore include other elements in the response to price.) Consider a farmer living at A; if the price at two available markets A and B are P_a and P_b respectively, and the transport cost incurred in travelling with the goods from A to B is y, then while $P_b - y > P_a$, marketing occurs at B. Once transport costs change so that $P_b - y' < P_a$, the demand for transport falls.

These individual cases indicate price thresholds. For a large number of employees, of shoppers or of marketing farmers the thresholds will vary. As a result the response of total demand to price changes will be gradual and can be expressed as a demand curve. It should be noted also that the alternative locations will not be present in all cases. In some cases there is no alternative, and still the demand for transport falls, as increasing transport cost reduces the incentive to work or buy, or to produce. In addition an employee's response to increased commuting costs may be to change his place of residence; and again the demand for transport falls.

The Transport of Commodities

The influence of transport costs on producers with specified supply curves can be illustrated from two types of primary production. In West Africa the peasant producer price of cocoa is based on prices in world markets such as New York and London minus transport and handling costs.[17] An increase in sea transport costs between

West Africa and these markets will therefore result in a reduced producer price. This reduction will be uniform within a single country, and may result in a fall in production, and the tonnage component in demand will decrease. In contrast an increase in overland transport costs within the country of production will have the greatest effect, in price terms and therefore in supply terms, on remote areas of production. Within the country the tonnage and distance components of demand will decrease.

A second illustration is provided in the supply, and thus the transport demand for iron ore. Manners has demonstrated the importance of the 'cost and freight' (c. and f.) price of iron ore at the blast furnace.[18] He records the dramatic fall in ocean freight rates for iron ore in the period 1955–65. 'Where a mining operation cannot make a profit out of a given pattern of cost and freight prices less the relevant transfer charges, that operation is priced out of the market.'[19] In a period of falling transport costs the richer, easily worked deposits compete more strongly, even where they are remote from their markets. As a result the mileage component of demand has increased in relative importance. Finally it is clear from the volume of cross-hauling of scarcely distinguishable products that all free enterprise systems (and probably all economic systems) have an element of inefficiency in the matching of suppliers and consumers. This excess ton-mileage probably constitutes an important part of the demand for transport. When the costs of transport are low the incentive to seek out and eliminate such inefficiency is low, but if transport costs are high that incentive is increased and the distance component of demand will be capable of some reduction.

These problems are such that many studies of transport demand (so-called) do no more than attempt to extrapolate trends or to interpret the elasticities from observed price–demand fluctuations. Although this method is acceptable in the preparation of policy, *faute de mieux*, it cannot be seen as a satisfactory methodological basis of explanation.

2.3 THE ECONOMIC ORGANISATION OF TRANSPORT DEMAND

The preceding sections drew attention to the spatial characteristics of transport demand, especially dispersion and concentration. A spatially dispersed demand may nevertheless be organised as a single customer for transport; this is a benefit of the cooperative organisation of farming. On the other hand a demand which is spatially concentrated may be organisationally fragmented among a large number of producers, consumers or trading intermediaries. The consequences of economic organisation, and especially of economies of scale, are recognised by many writers, and Chisholm notes that 'external economies arise from the provision of facilities, or the better use of what exists. This is particularly evident in the case of transport. . . .'[20] In addition larger units of production may be able to make more detailed investigation of transport problems in order to achieve the most satisfactory solution.

Less often recognised are the consequences of the scale of economic activity in transport demand. The transport operator's pattern of operations, his rating structure and his capital investment may all be affected by the size of consignments made by his customers.

Consignment Size and Economic Organisation

A traffic in small consignments will reflect the scale of operations by both consignor and consignee. It may also reflect demand schedules which require frequent small shipments rather than less frequent but larger ones. If these small shipments reflect conditions at both origin and destinations the situation is not easily changed. If on the other hand the small scale of operations is only at one end of the transport operation, a wholesaling, warehousing or depot system may allow the consolidation of the traffic over the greater part of the distance.

Small shipments have adverse effects upon the efficiency of the transport undertaking. In the first place, smaller shipments will, *ceteris paribus*, require a greater amount of packaging; this will increase the gross tonnage moved. Secondly, each consignment requires documentation: check weighing, waybills and invoices. The documentation will be greater on international routes in order to meet customs requirements. Such documentation is costly (it requires clerical labour and appropriate office facilities) and time-consuming (resulting in reduced transit speeds). Thirdly, small consignments will necessitate more handling per unit weight moved. This handling requires increased labour and heavy capital investment, and reduces transit speeds.

The economic impact of 'smalls' traffic is discussed in the Beeching

Report. Studies revealed that in 1961 British Railways carried 43 million consignments of 177 million packages. Average consignment weight was 178 lb, average package weight was 43 lb. 'Based on the study and detailed costing, the annual receipts were estimated to be £36m, and direct costs £47m, a loss of £11m taking no account of indirect expenses and interest charges.'[21] British Rail also have high costs from the investments necessary in the handling of small consignments. In 1961 approximately 57 per cent of mineral traffic and 81 per cent of the general merchandise moved in less than full train loads. These shipments are handled by large marshalling yards. They also contribute to the slow 'turn round' times of rolling stock. In 1961 'the average turn round time from loading to loading is 11·9 working days. The average loaded transit time is 1½–2 days'.[22]

Another example can be taken from air transport. The Paris Airport Authority plans a new international airport, 'Paris Nord', to be operational by 1972. At the new site they propose a freight area of 100 000 square metres of covered warehouses and 300 000 square metres of offices, an indication of the capital costs incurred by freight terminals.

Transporter Response to Small Consignment Size

The British Railways data illustrate the failure of receipts from small consignments to meet costs. A series of charges may be made to reduce this gap, or to discourage small shipments. A minimum charge can be made for all consignments below a certain weight, this charge representing the costs of documentation and handling. In some cases there may be a separate tariff for consignments below a specified size, a common practice of many port authorities and shipping lines.

Several attempts have been made to reduce documentation and its attendant expenditure and delay. In international trade this has been a concern of the Organisation for European Economic Co-operation, and in the United Kingdom of the National Economic Development Office. In this international traffic the standardisation of documents and the acceptance of advance customs clearance have an important part to play. For specific customers some operators may agree contract rates which reduce the documentation and handling of individual consignments. Such an approach is only possible where the customer is handling large tonnages.

The effects of high rates for small shipments, or related pressures, or the introduction of new transport technologies, may bring about structural changes in a traffic, an effective increase in consignment size. Such structural changes may be initiated by a consignor, a consignee or some trading intermediary. The most notable recent innovation of this type has resulted from the introduction of units and containers. The possibility of simplified documentation, reduced freight and insurance charges, and speedier transit has made the container load the most desirable minimum consignment size on many ocean shipping routes, and intermediary companies are being developed to assemble such container loads from a multiplicity of smaller shipments.

The study of consignments will be taken up again in a later section. Smith and Hay have argued that the size of consignments or 'strands' is an unjustly neglected feature of commodity flows.[23] Superficially similar flows may yet have different consignment patterns; different consignment patterns may influence the allocation of traffic to different transport media. The reasons for such differences will only be apparent in a careful study of the economic organisation of transport demand.

2.4 VARIATION IN DEMAND OVER TIME

Patterns of demand are not constant over time. Variations may occur in the total volume, in direction or in the distance and volume components of demand. The variations observed may follow a regular pattern, recurring over the day, the week or longer periods; on the other hand some are irregularly spaced in time. One problem is common for all such situations: adequate provision for all demands can only be ensured at the price of excess capacity at some periods; alternatively full utilisation of capacity can be achieved at the cost of leaving demands unsatisfied.

Regular Variations

In many cases the variation of demand follows a regular cycle, reflecting similar cycles in the level of economic activity. Often the underlying reason for the variation is some astronomical or meteorological phenomenon. For example, diurnal variations are usually linked to the hours of daylight, and patterns of shift working. The

greatest impact occurs in the demand for intra-urban transport by
the labour force. The variation usually exhibits marked peaks in
volume, and often a change of direction between peaks. A subsidiary
variation is often linked to the peak hours for school travelling and
retail shopping. During the hours of darkness all these demands will
be reduced, and may be totally absent.[24] The diurnal variation in
the demand for freight transport is less marked; but it is evident
that it too is affected by the pattern of working hours. In many cases
it is impossible to measure demand, as distinct from flows, in an
urban area. Estimates can however be prepared from data on work
place, residence, working hours and production.

Although the intra-urban case is most markedly affected by diurnal
variation, similar variations occur in the demand for passenger
transport on inter-urban and even international routes. The dis-
advantages of arrival or departure in the middle of the night are
evident, while on the other hand there may be an increased demand
for overnight travel on those routes where arrival in the early morning
is possible. This variation in demand affects both railway and air
passenger transport over long distances.

Weekly variations are also a widespread feature. Most societies
have a weekly cycle of activity which may include a market day
(and hence increased transport demand) and a rest day (with a de-
creased demand). Although a seven-day cycle is accepted in both
Christian and Muslim countries, other 'weeks' of four, five and eight
days occur. The response to such fluctuations in demand can be
detected in the provision of local bus services in the rural areas of
England.

Seasonal fluctuations in the demand for transport are most often
associated with the agricultural sector, but some service and manufacturing industries also exhibit such variations in demand. The
most acute case will occur in those agricultural economies where
activity is concentrated upon a single crop or a narrow range of similar
crops. The principal peak in demand will be associated with the crop
harvest, but there may be subsidiary peaks, as for example the distribution of fertiliser. In Nigeria, for example, the major demands for
transport arise from the great export crops: cocoa, palm produce,
groundnuts and cotton. All these have short harvest periods, and
for cocoa, groundnuts and cotton the transport demand is concentrated in the period from November to February.

The seasonal effect can also be noted in other demands for freight transport. The effect of weather on building operations leads to a decline in transport demand during spells of wet or cold weather. Such a variation can be observed in the United Kingdom. Again cold weather leads to seasonal variations in the consumption of heating fuels, which will result in seasonal peaks in transport demand. This latter pattern is a well-marked feature of the demand for oil tanker charters to Europe in the winter months. The combination of all these variations leads to an overall seasonality in transport demand.[25] In north-west Europe this is apparent in the graphs prepared by Bayliss,[26] and in the sample survey of road transport in the United Kingdom (table 2.2).

TABLE 2.2

ESTIMATED PROPORTION OF ROAD VEHICLES
IN THE UNITED KINGDOM
IDLE DURING EACH QUARTER OF 1962

| Licence type | *Percentages by quarters* | | | |
	Winter	Spring	Summer	Autumn
A	10	8	10	9
Contract A	17	9	11	8
B	14	10	14	10
C	16	8	12	11

Source: Ministry of Transport. Statistical Paper no. 2, *Survey of Road Goods Transport 1962, Final Results, Part I*, HMSO, London (1964), p. 57.

A similar seasonality can be observed in the demand for passenger transport. This is exemplified by the 'holiday traffic' in Great Britain. The overall seasonal peak is in July and August. At specific centres it may be concentrated within a particular holiday week or fortnight. The results of providing capacity to meet this demand were revealed in the Beeching Report on British Railways. Of the total available coaching stock the last 2000 coaches were only required on ten occasions, the preceding 2000 on fourteen occasions, and the preceding 2000 on fewer than eighteen occasions.[27] Seasonal peaks in passenger demand may however be present in the winter months—for example, to ski resorts and to areas of 'more fashionable' climate. They may also be international in character: thus the passenger demand on North Atlantic routes shows marked seasonality.[28]

It can be argued that the demand for transport is subject to long-term fluctuations of a cyclical nature. The identification of such variations, their relation to the 'trade cycle' and their effects upon transport operation have been discussed by both Isard[29] and Campbell.[30] The effects of long-term variation will be most marked in those transport industries where capital is fixed in facilities and stock which have long depreciation periods. The significance of all these regular variations for the present study lies in their influence upon the spatial patterns of networks and of flows.

Irregular Variations in Transport Demand

At the level of the individual producer, consumer or passenger, demand for transport will often be irregular. For example the demands of a single manufacturing plant may well reflect the week-to-week variations in the order book. A study of industrial demand for transport in Cumberland revealed the large number of such irregular consignments (table 2.3). This has important consequences for the

TABLE 2.3

THE REGULARITY OF CONSIGNMENTS BY
INDUSTRIAL ESTABLISHMENTS

Commodity	Percentages			
	Daily	*Weekly*	*Monthly*	*Irregular*
All commodities	51	23	10	16
of which:				
Metal manufacture	—	23	33	44
Building materials	35	22	8	35
Electrical and other				
machinery	36	24	16	24

Source: *West Cumberland Transport Survey, Statistical Appendix*, Northern Economic Planning Board, Newcastle (1967), p. 9.

routing of traffic and the choice of transport medium. Where a consignment is irregular the consignor is unlikely to perform detailed cost comparisons in each case, and so least-cost routing will not necessarily occur.

Such irregular variations at the level of the firm or individual are often mutually compensating in aggregate demand, but more important in this present context is irregular variation in the overall demand within an area. Such irregularities may be due to external influences such as weather, or to unpredictable changes within the producing or consuming sector, such as the impact of a technological innovation. Ideally any measure of such fluctuation should be able to exclude the effects of both cyclic variation and long-term trend.

This is a problem which has already been met in related fields; in climatology, rainfall variability may be expressed as relative variability, the index of variability or the coefficient of variation. The vices and virtues of such measures are discussed by Gregory.[31] In the field of international economics J. D. Coppock has been concerned with the variation in the supply and price of commodities entering international trade.[32] Coppock reviewed the available measures, the variance, the logarithmic variance and deviation from a best fit regression line. He finally developed an Instability Index which he described as 'a close approximation of the average year to year percentage variation adjusted for trend'.[33]

Three such measures of variation were used by the author to measure variation in the tonnage component of transport demand for cocoa in Western Nigeria from 1953–64. The measures were calculated for each of five producing areas which are ranked according to their scores on each measure in table 2.4. There is significant difference

TABLE 2.4

ANNUAL VARIATIONS IN THE TONNAGE OF COCOA
TO BE TRANSPORTED IN WESTERN NIGERIA, 1953–4

Rank	Variance	Long Variance	Coppock's Index
1	Oyo	Ijebu	Ijebu
2	Ondo	Oyo	Oyo
3	Ijebu	Ondo	Ondo
4	Abeokuta	Abeokuta	Abeokuta
5	Ibadan	Ibadan	Ibadan

Source: A. M. Hay. *Geography of Road Transport in Nigeria*, Ph.D. Thesis, Cambridge (1967), Appendix.

in the ranking between the variance and the other measures, largely due to the inability of the variance to eliminate the effects of expansion in Ondo and decline in Ijebu. Such indices of variation can be calculated and mapped, either for demand within an area, along a specific route or through transport nodes.

Another cruder method is applied to Nigerian port statistics in table 2.5. The actual tonnages handled each year are expressed as percentages of the five-year running mean. In a twelve-year period minor peak years are frequent, but greater peaks occur in the export (or agricultural) sector.

TABLE 2.5

ANNUAL VARIATIONS IN NIGERIAN PORT TRAFFIC, 1955–66
(BY VOLUME)

Percentage above 5-year mean	*Number of years*		
	All traffic	*Imports*	*Exports*
under 5	5	4	2
5–10	1	3	2
10–15	1	–	1
15–20	–	–	1
20–30	–	–	–
over 30	–	–	1

Source: Calculated from Nigerian Ports Authority statistics.

Compensating for Variation

It has already been noted that some variations in demand are mutually compensating, so that overall demand remains relatively constant. In many cases, however, variations in aggregate demand are present and the transport operator is faced with the problem of meeting peak demands and yet maintaining high load factors.

One method of achieving this is to match maximum demand against essential unutilised time. Thus staff holidays, and the servicing of vehicles, terminal facilities and track maintenance can be confined to off-peak periods. This approach is widely adopted in the maintenance and repair schedules for main lines on British Railways. Similarly the servicing of commuter buses can be confined to the period 10 a.m. to 4 p.m., and to the night shift. In some cases it is possible to lay up capacity, if the costs of laying up are less than the losses occasioned by continued operation with low load factors. This is a common response in ocean shipping: in 1967 the United States reserve merchant fleet alone totalled 1·75 million tons. Charging policy can be devised to penalise peak traffic and attract off-peak traffic. Such policy may be focused upon the timing of movement alone, or on the direction of movement at peak times.

2.5 URGENCY

The measures taken to 'spread' peak demand, and their success, are largely dependent upon the urgency of that demand. Where delay is enforced the demand may be diverted or reduced, or become more responsive to price. Three categories of such urgency can be distinguished: immediacy, perishability and interdependence.

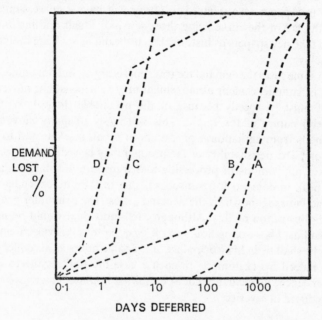

Fig. 2.4. The effect of delay on transport demand

Immediacy can be illustrated from the case of the daily newspaper. The demand for transport becomes effective when the first batch of copies leaves the press. Supply cannot anticipate demand. The demand continues at a high level until, say, 5 a.m. After that time it is too late for papers to reach the readers' breakfast tables; the demand cannot be postponed. A similar pattern exists with the passenger demand for transport to a holiday resort. Within his limited holiday period a traveller wishes to maximise his stay at the resort in question. Thus at both ends of the holiday his demand for transport is immediate.

In freight traffic the immediacy may not be so clearly expressed, but delayed orders may mean lost orders. The demand cannot be indefinitely postponed. This question of immediacy can be illustrated graphically, as in figure 2.4. The curves represent traffics with different immediacy patterns. Some traffics may be wholly indifferent to delay until a late date (A), others may be largely indifferent (B). On the other hand other demands may be extremely sensitive (C). The newspaper case referred to above will have a curve similar to D; the tail of the curve being those few individuals and institutions who take newspapers as historical records and as such are indifferent to delay.

In some cases the demand for transport is urgent but not immediate; that is, commencement of movement may be delayed but movement itself must be speedy because of the perishable (literally or figuratively) nature of the traffic. This will apply to many movements of foods from agricultural producers to urban markets and to processors. The perishability of the product may be reduced by technological innovations in processing and transport. In other instances the peak in demand for transport is due to the interdependence of the activities from which the demand arises. The commuter problem is an illustration of this. Although each individual would be happy to readjust his working hours to off-peak periods, his work demands that he shall be in his work-place at the same hours as his colleagues, and indeed his customers. In such a case the peak is due to interdependence; its incidence could be shifted in time, but cannot easily be reduced in severity.

2.6 TRENDS IN DEMAND

The long-term trend of aggregate transport demand is upward; but individual demands (for a commodity, at a point, within an area or along a route) vary in their rate of change; some may decrease. In many cases the long-term trend must be distinguished from shorter-term fluctuations of a regular or irregular type. The statistical methods available for such analyses are reviewed in standard texts.[34] The distinction must also be made between ratio and incremental rates of growth. For transport studies some additional distinctions become important.

Expansion in Transport Demand

An expansion of transport demand can be expected in a period of economic expansion, but it is necessary to distinguish between the distance and volume components of this trend. In some cases the increase is the result of increased production and consumption at established centres, and therefore only the volume of demand increases. Where however one of these activities is extensive in its use of land, both distance and volume components increase.[35] Thus for example the increase in cereal production in Canada in the nineteenth century involved an increase both in distance and in volume of transport demand.[36] The same pattern may occur within a conurbation: if population growth results in urban spread, with no compensating dispersion of job opportunities, both the number of potential passengers and the distance component of their transport demand increases. The extent to which this may occur has been dramatically underlined by Hall's study of *London 2000*.[37]

In a few cases the increase in transport demand may be the result of an increase in the distance component alone. This most commonly occurs when the sources of commodity supply are changed. Thus in many cases the exhaustion of a mineral deposit will lead to replacement from a remoter source. No change in volume is necessarily expected. Such a pattern was a recurrent feature of the early European iron and steel industry. In the early stages dependence on charcoal for reduction of the ore led to a rapid exhaustion of low-cost supplies near to the forges, and the iron masters were forced to bring supplies from further afield. A second phase occurred with the discovery of coke smelting; in that case, when local bog ores and coal measure ores were exhausted ore sources were developed at a distance.[38]

The component increases in transport demand may have important consequences for transport development. Where the demand increases in volume alone, provision can be made by increasing vehicle capacity and perhaps duplicating existing facilities. If however the increase has a large distance component, provision of increased network mileage may be necessary. The development of Canada's wheatlands necessitated an extension of the rail network, the expansion of conurbations necessitates increased route mileage of roads, railways and public transport services.

Contraction in Transport Demand

The same distinction between distance and volume components must be considered in the contraction of demand. Contraction in volume alone is the more common; it can for example be associated with industrial decline or depopulation. It is also the most serious for the transport operator. A complete network has to be maintained to handle diminishing traffic. This is the core of the 'rural transport problem' in the United Kingdom, where railways and bus services are expected to serve diminishing numbers of people over a great route mileage.[39]

In some cases the contraction in demand results from a contraction in the mileage component of demand only. For example, an industrial entrepreneur may 'discover' a source of raw material which, being nearer, allows him to reduce transport costs. Alternatively he may decide to relocate his plant at a point which minimises his transport costs, a common feature of many theories of plant location and migration. A final example may occur as a result of changed marketing policy, competition or changed market conditions. An entrepreneur is the only manufacturer of a product at A; he sells all his production within a hundred miles of A. Conditions change: either the market close to A expands, in which case he can ignore more distance markets and sell only in the closer markets where profits are higher; or the further markets are captured by competitors, forcing him to sell his product in the nearer markets. In both cases the transport demand is reduced in the distance component. A process of this kind has occurred in Nigeria from 1958 to 1965. The first cement plant was built in 1958 at Nkalagu in the eastern part of the country. In the succeeding years capacity was expanded and sales were extended to all parts of the country; transport demand was increased in both distance and volume. From 1960 however the mileage component was reduced as remoter parts of the market were subjected to competition from both imports and further Nigerian plants; total demand for transport declined despite an increase in the volume component.[40]

Indivisibilities in the Provision of Transport Capacity

Pragmatically the greatest problem posed by variations in demand over time is the contrast between the pattern of change and the pattern of provision. For most transport forms investment in new capacity is 'lumpy' because of 'indivisibilities'; that is, the increments of increased capacity are comparatively large. Thus, for example a new railway line represents an initial capacity of perhaps three-quarters of a million tons per annum in each direction. This capacity can be increased to a certain extent by increasing passing loops and improving schedules, but when maximum capacity is reached a second line must be laid to increase capacity further. As a result

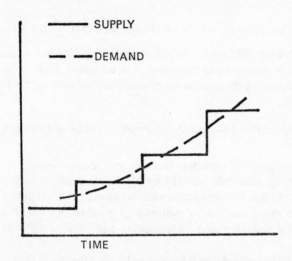

Fig. 2.5. Secular trend in demand and indivisibilities in supply

capacity increases in a stepped manner, as in figure 2.5. In contrast, increments of demand tend to be smaller and more frequent. They are represented as a smooth curve in figure 2.5. There is, therefore, a choice of strategies in matching the provision of capacity to demand. In the first, capacity always exceeds demand; the price paid is a low level of utilisation. In the second strategy, capacity lags behind demand, and a high level of utilisation is assured but demand is left unsatisfied. This surplus demand may be met by a competing route or transport medium. Intermediate solutions will carry both penalties, but to a lesser degree.

This question of indivisibilities has great importance for the developing countries. Although the absolute excess of demand over capacity or *vice versa* remains the same for each time period, its relative importance is greatest at the initial period. Secondly, it can be argued, as for example by Hirschmann,[41] that transport is a 'leading sector' and excess capacity will generate demand. On the other hand, a transport shortage or bottleneck will retard growth in other sectors and thus the overall demand for transport. For these reasons it is often argued that investment in transport, even far in excess of current demand, is justified as a development strategy.

2.7 THE IMPACT OF TRANSPORT PROVISION ON DEMAND

In discussing changes in the nature and magnitude of demand over time, it is necessary to recognise that transport demand may itself be influenced by the installation of transport facilities and the provision of service.

Transport Provision and the Changing Location of Economic Activity

The installation of transport facilities may lead to changed locational patterns of economic activity by a relocation of existing activities or by a change in comparative rates of growth. Although this change will be most marked in patterns of production, other activities including residence and consumption can also be affected in this way.

On an international or interregional scale, changes in the location of production can be interpreted by the law of comparative advantage,[42] or in the terms suggested in figures 2.2 and 2.3 above. But it must be noted that such analyses are only valid in the short run, because in the long run the factor costs of production are not necessarily independent of transport flows. It is for this reason that an analysis based on spatial price interdependence must be used for long-range prediction of the impact of transport investment on demand.

On a local scale the changing locations will result in new spatial arrangements of transport demand, particularly its degree of spatial concentration or dispersal. The nature of the change will often depend on the nature of the new facilities. A transport facility with limited access will encourage the clustering of demand around the access points; a facility with unlimited access may lead to a greater dispersal or perhaps to a linear shaping of the pattern. These changes can be illustrated from the growth of suburbs as affected by suburban transport services. Railways have tended to lead to pockets of clustered urban development, buses have encouraged linear or ribbon development, while private vehicle ownership has encouraged a formerly undreamed-of dispersal of transport demand. A similar sequence can be observed in industrial locations within the city: initial locations or nineteenth-century relocations tended to cluster along canals and railways. It is only the advent of the motor vehicle which has allowed the dispersal of industry to peripheral industrial estates.[43]

Effects on the Economic Organisation of Demand

The role of the wholesaler in concentrating demand for transport has already been noted. If new facilities offer transport only to the specialist, perhaps with investment in vehicles, the wholesaler is well placed to take on this additional role. If however the new facility is open to all potential customers, regardless of consignment size, the role of the wholesaler may well be replaced by direct consignment.

3 Elementary Description of Transport Networks

The elementary description of transport networks includes two categories of analysis, morphological and functional. The morphological approach focuses upon those characteristics of network form which are recognised intuitively to be important, for example accessibility and orientation. The functional study is based upon the dominant pattern of network use.

3.1 ELEMENTARY MORPHOLOGICAL PROPERTIES OF TRANSPORT NETWORKS

The pattern of transport facilities has a double importance in the present context. In the first place the networks are themselves important features of the geographic and economic landscapes deserving description, measurement and explanation. In the second place the network is a determinant of the pattern of transport flows. The description of network form has long been a topic of interest to geographers[1] and economists,[2] but despite these efforts neither precise measurement nor a satisfactory taxonomy has been achieved. For example, the concept of network orientation is intuitively reasonable, true to experience, and therefore widely used in verbal description. It is however of limited comparative value (over space or time) because of its subjective nature. There are two approaches to this problem. The first is to posit an ideal transport surface and to measure all network qualities as deviations from this ideal—distortions of the uniform transport surface. Such an approach is rooted in empirical observation and map analysis. The other approach seeks to define the relation between intuitive notions and abstract mathematical properties of the networks (chapter 4).

The Uniform Transport Surface and its Distortions

The uniform transport surface is defined as an area in which the movement of goods and persons is equally easy and cheap at all points, over all distances and in all directions. Such a concept was originally devised as a simplifying assumption in location theory,[3] but it is used here to define an ideal situation from which deviations can be observed.

The properties of this surface can be defined as follows:

(*i*) an infinite number of available routes is present (in other words, the route density is infinitely high);

(*ii*) a single variable (geodetic distance) will alone determine the time, effort and cost of movement between any two points (there is no orientation);

(*iii*) all locations can be reached directly from all other locations (total connectivity exists);

(*iv*) movement can be initiated at any point within the area (total accessibility);

(*v*) the surface is homogeneous at all geographical scales (strictly speaking this definition is subsumed in definitions *i–iv*).

The uniformity of the surface is initially distorted by natural features, a distortion which occurs even on those surfaces which appear at first sight to be homogeneous, such as the ocean. The processes of human settlement lead to an increasing heterogeneity of the surface. Human activities such as land ownership and building lead to reduced mobility in certain areas and in certain directions. Route construction itself distorts the uniform transport surface in two ways. Firstly, it is intended to create lines of communication which are distinguished by greater ease of movement, cheapness or speed. An indirect second effect is often to inhibit transverse movements: thus railways and motorways become barriers to movement.

Network Density and Allied Properties

The simplest measure of route construction is route density (linear units of route per unit area). Such measures have been widely employed for comparisons between nations, within nations and even between small localities. They do however have severe limitations. Some of these are a problem of definition. For example, in recording railway statistics it is necessary to distinguish between route mileage and track mileage. In studies of road networks it is difficult to ensure that roads of similar status are recorded in comparable fashion in all the study areas. Other problems involved are more serious. All such measures involve a degree of generalisation implicit in areal averages. This is insignificant if the accounting units are small but becomes acute where large areal units such as nations are involved. A more acute problem still is the fact that there is no necessary relation

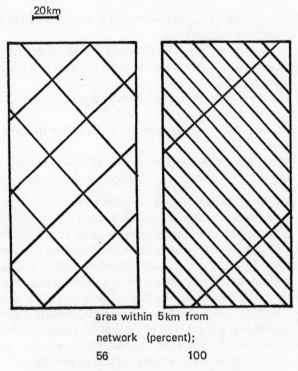

20km

area within 5 km from

network (percent);

56   100

Fig. 3.1. Some elementary network properties

between route density and the intuitive concept of connectivity. This is simply illustrated for the units in figure 3.1. The same figure can be used to illustrate a further network property; the proportion of the area within a given distance of the network. This statistic was used by Jefferson in his pioneer paper on railway networks.[4] He mapped the range of these indices for the rail routes of the world and identified two types: railwebs and railnets. He defined railwebs as those where the whole area served is within ten miles of the network; in a railnet major parts of the area lie beyond this limit. Jefferson identified

150 miles per thousand square miles as the threshold density at which railnets commonly become railwebs. The empirical regularity noted by Jefferson has a clearly defined geometric basis (which he did not

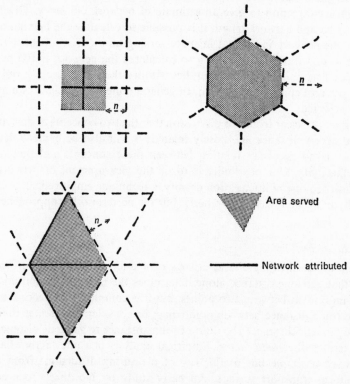

Fig. 3.2. Access distance in three regular networks

explore). Three types of totally regular networks are possible (figure 3.2) and for all of these a simple relation holds.[5]

$$D = L A^{-1} = n^{-1}$$

where A = area under study
L = length of network
D = network density
n = maximum distance of any point in the area from the network.

Thus in Jefferson's example, with a value of n equalling ten miles, the density expected is one-tenth, or 100 miles per 1000 square miles. The difference between this result and Jefferson's data can be attributed to irregularities in the network. The formula can also be used in the contrary direction to give an estimate of network efficiency. Given the area and network length it is possible to calculate the maximum n if the network is efficient in space serving terms. If all of the area lies at or within the value of n so calculated the network is 100 per cent efficient, if only 70 per cent lies within n then the network is only 70 per cent efficient, and so on. In general quite low efficiencies may be expected.

It will be clear from this discussion that the two concepts of density and access distance are closely related; it will also be evident that there is no necessary relation between these concepts and that of connectivity. One possibility is to tie the measurement of network density to one of intersection density, a technique employed successfully in urban areas by Borchert,[6] but the need for other approaches is evident.

Route Factors

One of the defining characteristics of a uniform transport surface is that geodetic distance alone determines the time, effort and cost of movement between two points, but it is common experience that the route distance between points may be considerably greater than the geodetic distance. The ratio of route distance to geodetic distance is termed the *route factor*. Empirical analysis of route factors has proved a simple but useful way of measuring distortions from a uniform transport surface. An early study by Nordbeck focused upon the routes within towns,[7] later studies have looked at nation-wide patterns in the United Kingdom[8,9] and Poland,[10] and international contrasts have been examined in West Africa.[11] There have in addition been a few route factor studies incidental to studies of location.[12]

The route factor is calculated for a number of origin–destination pairs. In most published studies these pairs have been purposively selected but random selection could equally well be employed. From these data it is possible to calculate the average route factor in the network and its standard deviation; an alternative method uses linear regression to specify the relation between route distance and geodetic distance, and the coefficient of determination can then be used as a measure of variation. The first method yields an average route factor of 1·25 in the United Kingdom,[13] but higher figures have been observed elsewhere, for example in three West African countries.[14]

The average route factor resulting from such measurement will usually have two components. The first component is due to deviations on the individual routes: the sum of minor deviations caused by the need to avoid obstacles. Timbers found that in the United Kingdom this averaged about 1·08 over five-mile stretches of road.[15] A second component is due to the structure of the network. Holroyd has calculated the average route factor which may be expected in networks of regular geometry, but in which all individual links are straight, as 1·27 for both square and hexagonal networks but 1·10 for a sixty degree triangular network,[16] suggesting that in this respect triangular networks are superior to the alternative regular forms. A third element present in some studies is the irregular shape of the area studied. It can be inferred from the work of Timbers that the indentations of the United Kingdom coastline alone would have resulted in an average route factor of 1·08.[17] If the three components are multiplied (1·08 for route deviation, 1·10 for a triangular network, and 1·08 for irregularity of the coastline) the product of 1·28 is not inconsistent with the overall average of 1·25.

An alternative use of the route factor is to test for the presence of certain intuitively recognised network characteristics. For example, it is often asserted that a network shows marked orientation towards specified nodes or regions; if this orientation exists it should be reflected in markedly lower route factors. An examination of three West African networks in this fashion revealed little evidence of orientation, and such as there is appears to be towards unexpected locations: not ports or metropolises but inland towns.[18]

Access Points

In most transport systems access to the network is determined not by route mileage but by the limited number of access points. The chief exceptions to this rule are those road networks where access is almost unlimited and in proportion to route mileage, but for railways, sea and air transport access points are the critical feature. Once again it is possible to identify optimal configurations and to define the density implied by an access criterion, in the form 'no point is more than n miles from an access point'. The optimal distribution of access points is a lattice of 60 degree triangles, with the centre of each n miles from the apices, where each apex is an access point serving a hexagonal area. The area of such a hexagon is then approximately $2 \cdot 6n^2$, and the density of access points is a reciprocal of this figure. The relation between access and access point density is similar to that shown in figure 3.2, and it is clear that the triangular arrangement is superior to the regular grid square alternative.

The pattern of access points within an area can be examined in the same manner as the pattern of routes. The density of access points is measured. This value again implies a maximum access distance (n) if the optimal pattern of location is present. The proportion of the area lying beyond this access distance can then be considered as a measure of the extent to which the transport surface lacks efficiency in supplying general accessibility. An analysis of this type is presented in table 3.1. The data for railway stations in Paris are taken

TABLE 3.1

EXAMPLES OF ACCESS POINT DENSITY AND ACCESSIBILITY

Transport medium	Area	Density	Access distance	Percentage of area beyond access distance
Railway[a]	Paris (5–9·99 miles)	0·429	0·949	c. 40
Airport	State of Wisconsin	0·002	15·031	c. 5

[a] D. S. Neft. Some aspects of rail commuting: New York, London, Paris. *Geographical Review*, 49 (1959), p. 159.

from Neft's comparative study of rail accessibility in three metropolitan areas.[19] The data for the second study were prepared by the author from State of Wisconsin records of licensed airports.[20] Examination of this result suggests that the Wisconsin airports approach the optimal triangular lattice pattern.

This finding can be further tested by using the nearest neighbour statistic.[21] This statistic ranges from 0 (total concentration) through

1 (random pattern) to 2·15 (the maximum dispersal of a triangular lattice). The statistic was applied to ten randomly located quadrats of 900 square miles, and the results are tabulated in table 3.2; in

TABLE 3.2

NEAREST NEIGHBOUR TESTS ON THE SPACING
OF WISCONSIN AIRPORTS

Quadrat	Number of airports	Nearest neighbour statistic
I	2	1·28
II	3	1·83
III	22	0·77
IV	2	1·79
V	3	1·58
VI	3	1·14
VII	2	1·28
VIII	2	1·28
IX	2	1·54
X	2	1·28

Source: see text.

eight of the ten quadrats the degree of spacing was greater than random.

It is evident that the spacing of railway stations will be strongly influenced by the pattern of routes. It may therefore be of interest to examine the frequency of access points along a line rather than in an area. This type of analysis can identify quite important differences between networks, or in the same network at different time periods. The British Rail network for example shows clear regional contrasts in the frequency of access points between the Southern Region (commuter lines) and the Western Region (rural lines). There is also evidence that the 'Beeching era' was one not only of decreasing route mileage but also of decreasing access to that mileage. The same type of analysis might be used to examine the spacing of ports on a coastline or a river and the spacing of junctions on a motorway.

The testing for significance in these spacing patterns has proved of greater statistical complexity than might be supposed. An early study by Dacey of the spacing of river towns on the Mississippi used the concept of reflexive pairs.[22] In a reflexive pair each point's nearest neighbour itself has that point as nearest neighbour. The expected proportion of reflexive pairs (under randomness for a given number of points) of nth order nearest neighbour is given by $(\frac{2}{3})^n$. If the observed number of reflexive pairs is greater than expected the distribution tends to a uniform spacing; in the inverse case the points may be considered grouped. The same problem is briefly reviewed by King[23] but the solutions have not been widely applied in geography.[24]

3.2 FUNCTIONAL CLASSIFICATION OF NETWORK FACILITIES

The tools of measurement outlined in the preceding section allow a classification of whole networks, of nodes and of individual links on the basis of morphology. In some cases morphology and intended function is linked in a descriptive or prescriptive terminology (as for example trunk roads, ring roads). A pure functional classification on the other hand will be based upon the functions which the facilities actually perform at the period of analysis. In transport studies functional classification may be based on the magnitude of the traffic handled, on the geographical characteristics of the traffic handled or on the composition of the traffic.

Traffic Magnitudes

In studies of traffic magnitude three problems commonly present themselves: data selection, data aggregation, and problems of cartographic presentation. The first of these problems is illustrated by Rimmer's study of New Zealand seaports. He was concerned to identify the best summary measure of the status of these ports, and identified a number of possible measures including net registered tonnage of vessels using the port, total cargo handled, range of commodities handled and number of vessels entering, all for a given time period. Each of these measures yielded a slightly different ranking of New Zealand seaports but Rimmer concluded that cargo tonnage was the most satisfactory single measure.[25] A second problem occurs even after accepting Rimmer's conclusions when different commodities are measured in widely different units. For example shipping statistics are frequently given in shipping tons, or in tons weight, but other commodities may have quite different units of measurement—for example timber may be recorded in cubic feet. A similar problem arises in transport studies where a conversion factor is necessary to standardise statistics for different types of vehicle.[26] The problem becomes almost completely intractable when there are appreciable volumes of both freight and passenger traffic.

Surprisingly little work has been done in this field by geographers, but an interesting approach has been developed by Wallace[27] and followed by Turton.[28] Suppose all facilities (routes or access points) are grouped according to traffic volume in a cumulative frequency curve. It quickly becomes clear that in many cases a very small proportion of the network carries a large proportion of the traffic. This was made clear in the Beeching report on British Railways,[29] and the work of Turton suggests that this state of affairs has been present on the British railway network for many years.[30] A similar conclusion can be drawn from evidence on roads and ports. These same figures illustrate a problem of cartographic presentation: the use of a proportional line symbol is made difficult by the wide range of values. An ingenious attempt to solve the problem is made by Christensen using lines of standard width but with differing intensities of shading to indicate differences in volume.[31] The selection of suitable class intervals then occurs, but this is common to many forms of statistical mapping.

Geographical Characteristics

The use of geographical characteristics of traffic in the functional classification of network facilities has for a long time been used in the discussion of ports. Carter, for example, classified the ports of the United States into three categories—import, export and balanced traffic[32]—but it is necessary to distinguish also the trans-shipment function which is dominant at some large ports.

A similar approach was suggested by Wallace for the functional classification of railways.[33] He suggested that in addition to a functional role based on network form, for example the distinction between branch lines and trunk lines, it is possible to classify routes according to the direction of traffic. For example he distinguishes three types of branch line: those originating traffic, those with predominantly terminating traffic and those with balanced traffic. This type of analysis proved useful in a study of the railways in Australia and New Zealand; it has been applied by Wallace in the United States[34] and by Turton in the United Kingdom.[35] This last application appears to have had less success. The main reason for this is that in a geographically complex economy most links will have both originating and terminating traffic and only a few lines will be distinguished, for example routes serving the UK coalfields and routes serving an import or export port. Although these ideas are used intuitively about other forms of network facility, it is not clear whether they are used descriptively or prescriptively, and the categories in any case appear to be of limited usefulness.

Finally note can be taken of a refinement of the technique applied by Britton[36] and Bird[37] to port studies. The technique employs the 'location quotient', a widely used but rather unsatisfactory statistic. The simplest example can be stated in the following terms: suppose a port has 20 per cent of a nation's total traffic (inwards and outwards) but only 13 per cent of its inward traffic and 29 per cent of outward traffic. Then its location quotient for inward traffic would be 13/20 or 0·65 and its location quotient for outward traffic 29/20 or 1·45. The same technique can be applied according to broad destination regions. Suppose a United Kingdom port carries 15 per cent of total exports, but 24 per cent of exports to the USA and only 10 per cent of exports to Europe and 5 per cent of exports to Asia: the location quotients would then be 1·6 (USA), 0·67 (Europe) and 0·33 (Asia). Bird uses it to distinguish between ports with a world-wide function (London, Liverpool, Manchester, Bristol and the Clyde) and those with specialised functions (Grangemouth, Leith, Tyne and Cardiff).[38] The statistic must however be interpreted with caution, as it is not a significance statistic and there is a tendency for it to be high where the total percentages are low and *vice versa*.[39]

Traffic Type

Finally facilities may be classified by the type of traffic which they handle. Largely because of data problems, little use has been made of this approach, but it is possible to refer again to the work of Carter who noted that of sixty major US ports, thirty-one were dominated by petroleum traffic, eleven by iron ore and nine by coal.[40] This dominance may well be common to most port systems.

Conclusion

It will be clear that the functional classification of network facilities is beset by a number of procedural difficulties. The results of classification have not been very fruitful. Their potential importance in wedding the analysis of transport networks to the analysis of transport flows has not yet been realised and the approach remains excessively arid.

4 Topological Approaches to Network Form

The empirical approaches suggested in the preceding chapter have failed to provide adequate comparative measures of network characteristics which are intuitively and practically acknowledged to be important. An alternative approach has been devoted to the identification of topological properties defined in either the language of graph theory or the language of matrix algebra. The approach was pioneered by Garrison and Marble but the first systematic geographical application is due to Kansky.[1-3]

4.1 GRAPH THEORETIC APPROACHES TO NETWORK FORM

A transportation network can be simplified to retain essential topological characteristics but to exclude incidental characteristics. A simplification of this type is shown in figure 4.1. A number of properties are then defined.

(*i*) Each terminus and each route junction is termed a *vertex*. In the figures these are numbered v_1, v_2, etc. The term v (without a subscript) indicates the number of vertices.

(*ii*) Between certain of these vertices there are direct routes termed *edges*. The term e (without a subscript) denotes the number of edges.

(*iii*) It is possible to identify the number of subsidiary networks or *subgraphs* present (in the diagram this is evidently one) and this value is subsequently referred to as p.

These three definitions then become the basis for a series of measures both of the network as a whole, and of the status of individual vertices upon the network.

Derived Measures of Network Form

The first group of measures are termed by Kansky non-ratio measures. The first is termed the cyclomatic number, μ, and is derived from the equation

$$\mu = e - v + p \qquad (4.1)$$

Its most important function is to identify trees and disconnected graphs where p is greater than one. For all such networks μ equals

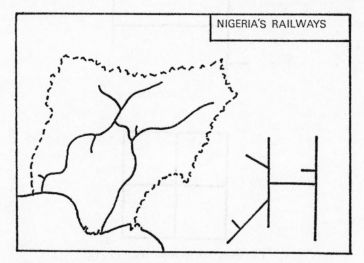

Fig. 4.1. The interpretation of a transport network as a graph

zero and for all other networks it will equal a positive whole number. The second measure is the diameter (δ) of the network, defined as 'the maximum number of edges in the shortest path between each pair of vertices'.[4] As shown in figure 4.2 this is in some respects a weak measure, failing to distinguish between graphs of very different form.

The second group of measures are ratio measures. The first of these, α, is a stronger form of the μ measure.

$$\alpha = \mu(2v - 5)^{-1} \qquad (4.2)$$

The dividend in this equation is μ while the divisor defines the maximum possible number of circuits for a stated number of vertices.

Values of α lie between one (maximum connectivity) and zero (failure to achieve connectivity, as is the case with disconnected graphs and trees). The β index is defined by the equation

$$\beta = ev^{-1} \tag{4.3}$$

The range of the index is from zero to three; trees and disconnected graphs have a β value less than one, a value of one identifies single

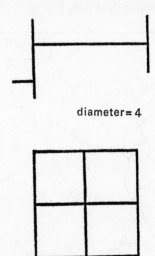

diameter = 4

Fig. 4.2. The diameter as a measure of graph form

circuit networks, and values greater than one identify the more complex networks.

The final measure, γ, is derived as

$$\gamma = e(3v - 6)^{-1} \tag{4.4}$$

In this equation the divisor indicates the maximum number of edges possible in a network with a given number of vertices and no duplicate routes. The values derived lie between zero and one but can be re-expressed as percentages (achieved connection as a percentage of maximum possible connection).

It is evident that all these measures are abstract in that the geographical magnitude of the network is ignored when all edges are arbitrarily assigned the value of one, but two further measures used by Kansky do incorporate the route distances.[5] The first is a measure of average edge length, η

$$\eta = Me^{-1} \qquad (4.5)$$

where M is the total network length. The π index is derived from the equation

$$\pi = Md^{-1} \qquad (4.6)$$

where M is the total route length and d the length of the network's diameter as defined above. The measure can be seen as indicating

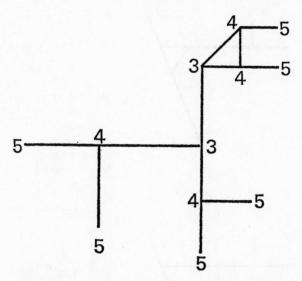

Fig. 4.3. The associated number of vertices in a graph

the compactness of the network. High values will indicate tightly knit networks, while low values will indicate straggling ill-connected networks. It is evident that the index can never have a value of less than one.

Finally Kansky identified some measures which could be used to describe the status of individual nodes within a network. For example the König or associated number expresses the maximum number of edges between a vertex and the most remote of the other vertices; it is thus a measure of the centrality of a vertex[6] (figure 4.3).

These and other measures have been the basis of empirical investigations by Kansky and others. The measures can be used to compare networks at different times or in different places. Many, too, allow topological comparison between networks at very different geographical scale. Before discussing this range of applications an evaluation of the measures is appropriate.

An Evaluation of Graph Theoretic Measures

The first major problem in the use of these measures is the definition of graph, edge and vertex. Graphs are usually divided into two groups:

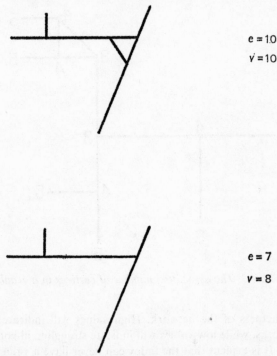

$e = 10$

$v = 10$

$e = 7$

$v = 8$

Fig. 4.4. Two graph interpretations of a three-way junction

planar and non-planar. In planar graphs (that is, graphs in a single plane) all intersections between edges are junctions and thus are counted as vertices. If on the other hand edges can cross without any junction, as for example in some railway systems, the graph is

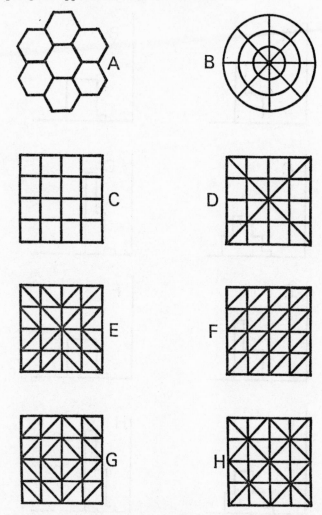

Fig. 4.5. The ideal networks examined by Werner's seminar
(after Werner)

non-planar. It is clear that most road and rail networks are planar but that some rail networks, such as London's rail system, and all airline networks are non-planar. The importance of this rule is that the formulae given above, which are for planar networks, must be

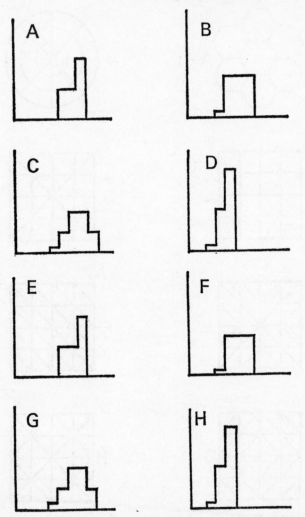

Fig. 4.6. Associated number distributions for ideal networks
(after Werner)

changed for non-planar networks (in the case of α and γ) while the
interpretation also differs in some cases (notably β). A similar problem
occurs with the definition of vertices. In strict terms an access point
on a straight line route, however important it may be, is not a vertex,

while the most trivial junction is. The problem arises in acute form with triangular junctions which may be variously interpretable as three vertices with three edges or as a single vertex with no edges (figure 4.4).

Quite a different point will be examined further in the next section, but it can be noted from the definitions that α, γ, β and μ are all linear combinations of three variables (e, v and p). It would be surprising if some of these measures were not redundant. The diameter, π and η indices, on the other hand, are independent.

An empirical evaluation of the measures was made by Werner and his associates.[7] They constructed a set of geometric networks which are shown in figure 4.5. They recorded that the two measures α and β were unable to discriminate between networks E, F, G and H. When they were used to rank the networks the measures all gave the ranking A, B, C, D and (together) E, F, G and H, suggesting that at least two of the measures are redundant. The γ measure ranks the networks in reverse order to α and β and again is unable to discriminate between E, F, G and H. The diameter measure picks out the large number of edges in A, C, F and G. For these reasons Werner sought for more discriminating uses of the graph theory concepts. Perhaps the most successful was his use of the associated number of the vertices to construct a frequency distribution for each network, as shown in figure 4.6.[8] The means and variances of the associated number were then calculated for each network. This procedure still failed to discriminate between three networks D, E and H.

Although some scholars are continuing to follow this line of investigation there must remain severe doubts as to whether the logical abstractions of graph theory at this simple level will ever be proved applicable to the geographical study of transport networks.

Empirical Applications of Graph Theoretic Measures

The failure of such investigations to recommend these indices is disappointing, for they had appeared to offer powerful tools of measurement in a comparative regional and comparative historical context. Kansky, for example, reports an investigation of both rail and road networks in twenty-five countries. The indices appeared to discriminate between networks, as is suggested by the rankings shown in table 4.1. Substantial agreement in ranking was shown by

TABLE 4.1

THE RAILWAY NETWORKS OF THIRTEEN COUNTRIES
RANKED BY GRAPH THEORETIC MEASURES

Rank	η	β	π
1	Nigeria	Angola	Ghana
2	Sudan	Ceylon	Chile
3	Iran	Iran	Iraq
4	Angola	Bolivia	Iran
5	Thailand	Ghana	Bolivia
6	Bolivia	Malaya	Angola
7	Mexico	Iraq	Malaya
8	Ceylon	Nigeria	Thailand
9	Turkey	Sudan	Nigeria
10	Iraq	Thailand	Sudan
11	Ghana	Turkey	Ceylon
12	Malaya	Mexico	Turkey
13	Chile	Chile	Mexico

Source: Derived from Kansky (*op. cit.* in text), tables 3 and 8.

TABLE 4.2

THE CORRELATION COEFFICIENTS BETWEEN GRAPH
THEORETIC MEASURES APPLIED TO THE RAIL AND ROAD
NETWORKS OF TWENTY-FIVE COUNTRIES

		Rail network			Road network
		β	η	π	β
Rail network	η	−0·68	—	—	—
	π	0·73	0·80	—	—
Road network	β	0·02	0·07	0·38	—
	η	−0·59	−0·57	−0·58	−0·37

Source: Kansky (*op. cit.* in text), table 14.

the various indices, but not such close agreement as to imply that some of the measures are redundant. Another result of Kansky's investigation is given in table 4.2.[9] It is clear that the graph theoretic measures derived for the networks of twenty-five countries can be used to perform a correlation analysis. The simple correlation coefficients measure the degree of association between pairs of network measures, a value of one implying complete association (and indicating some degree of redundancy) and a value of zero indicating complete lack of agreement. An examination of the table supports the autonomy of the β, η and π indices. It also indicates that there is no general association between the indices for the rail network and those for the road network. This is clearly brought out in row four of the correlation matrix.

The indices also appear to identify changes in the structure of a single network over time. Yeates[10] used data from Gould's[11] study

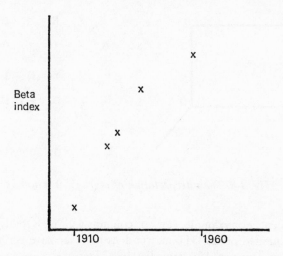

*Fig. 4.7. The primary and secondary road networks of Ghana:
beta index, 1910–59 (after Yeates)*

of Ghana to illustrate the development of that country's road network between 1910 and 1959. The values of the β index are shown on a graph in figure 4.7. The index identifies periods of greatly increased connectivity (1910–20 and 1927–37) and other periods in which the connectivity showed little significant change.

It is evident from the work of Kansky and those who have used his techniques that these indices have some descriptive and analytical value. Werner, on the other hand, has demonstrated that they need further appraisal, continued refinement and careful application.

4.2. MATRIX APPROACHES TO NETWORK FORMS

A closely allied group of studies has been based upon the use of matrix algebra. This depends upon the simplification of the network, in a manner analogous to graph theory, to form a binary connectivity matrix. This is an origin and destination table in which all towns, terminals and junctions are listed as origins and destinations. The presence of a direct link between the two points is identified by a one in the table, its absence by a zero (see figure 4.8). This C matrix can then be subjected to investigation. Some of its properties are

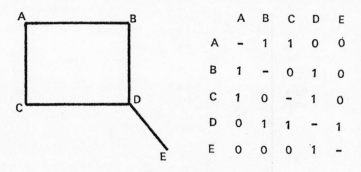

	A	B	C	D	E
A	-	1	1	0	0
B	1	-	0	1	0
C	1	0	-	1	0
D	0	1	1	-	1
E	0	0	0	1	-

Fig. 4.8. The interpretation of a graph as a matrix

self-evident. For example, rows or columns with high totals indicate well-connected nodes. The matrix does however have certain other properties which are less immediately evident.

Powering Binary Connectivity Matrices

If a connectivity matrix is raised to the power n, the entry in a given cell ($x_{ij} = c$) indicates that there are c possible ways to reach place i from place i in n steps. Further, *if* the network can be raised to the power n such that no cell has the value zero (this is called the solution matrix), the value n *may* then indicate the maximum number of steps between any two places on the network (that is, the diameter). The sequence of powered matrices can then be used for further analysis ($C^1, C^2, \ldots C^n$). The simplest form is the matrix T, where

$$T_n = C^1 + C^2 + \ldots + C^n \tag{4.7}$$

In the matrix T_n the row and column totals can be interpreted as indices of accessibility of the respective nodes. These values were identified by Garrison and used by Pitts to indicate the changing accessibility over time of towns in the Moscow basin.[12] A simple example is given in table 4.3.

TABLE 4.3

POWERING PROCEDURES APPLIED
TO THE CONNECTIVITY MATRIX IN FIGURE 4.8

$$C^2 = \begin{matrix} 2 & 0 & 0 & 2 & 0 \\ 0 & 2 & 2 & 0 & 1 \\ 0 & 2 & 2 & 0 & 1 \\ 2 & 0 & 0 & 3 & 0 \\ 0 & 1 & 1 & 0 & 1 \end{matrix} \qquad C^3 = \begin{matrix} 0 & 4 & 4 & 0 & 2 \\ 4 & 0 & 0 & 5 & 0 \\ 4 & 0 & 0 & 5 & 0 \\ 0 & 5 & 5 & 0 & 3 \\ 2 & 0 & 0 & 3 & 0 \end{matrix}$$

No solution matrix exists.

$$T_n = \begin{matrix} 2 & 5 & 5 & 2 & 2 \\ 5 & 2 & 2 & 6 & 1 \\ 5 & 2 & 2 & 6 & 1 \\ 2 & 6 & 6 & 3 & 4 \\ 2 & 1 & 1 & 4 & 1 \end{matrix} \qquad D_n = \begin{matrix} 0 & 1 & 1 & 2 & 3 \\ 1 & 0 & 2 & 1 & 2 \\ 1 & 2 & 0 & 1 & 2 \\ 2 & 1 & 1 & 0 & 1 \\ 3 & 2 & 2 & 1 & 0 \end{matrix}$$

Σ 16   16   16   21   9 $S =$ 7   6   6   5   8

For S: mean $= 6\cdot40$, variance $= 1\cdot04$
For d_{ij}: mean $= 1\cdot28$, variance $= 0\cdot94$

$$a^1C^1 = \begin{matrix} 0 & 0\cdot50 & 0\cdot50 & 0 & 0 \\ 0\cdot50 & 0 & 0 & 0\cdot50 & 0 \\ 0\cdot50 & 0 & 0 & 0\cdot50 & 0 \\ 0 & 0\cdot50 & 0\cdot50 & 0 & 0\cdot50 \\ 0 & 0 & 0 & 0\cdot50 & 0 \end{matrix} \qquad a^2C^2 = \begin{matrix} 0\cdot50 & 0 & 0 & 0\cdot50 & 0 \\ 0 & 0\cdot50 & 0\cdot50 & 0 & 0\cdot25 \\ 0 & 0\cdot50 & 0\cdot50 & 0 & 0\cdot25 \\ 0\cdot50 & 0 & 0 & 0\cdot75 & 0 \\ 0 & 0\cdot25 & 0\cdot25 & 0 & 0\cdot25 \end{matrix}$$

$$a^3C^3 = \begin{matrix} 0 & 0\cdot50 & 0\cdot50 & 0 & 0\cdot25 \\ 0\cdot50 & 0 & 0 & 0\cdot625 & 0 \\ 0\cdot50 & 0 & 0 & 0\cdot625 & 0 \\ 0 & 0\cdot625 & 0\cdot625 & 0 & 0\cdot375 \\ 0\cdot25 & 0 & 0 & 0\cdot375 & 0 \end{matrix} \qquad \begin{matrix} acT_n = \\ (n = 3) \end{matrix} \begin{matrix} 0\cdot50 & 1\cdot00 & 1\cdot00 & 0\cdot50 & 0\cdot25 \\ 1\cdot00 & 0\cdot50 & 0\cdot50 & 1\cdot125 & 0\cdot25 \\ 1\cdot00 & 0\cdot50 & 0\cdot50 & 1\cdot125 & 0\cdot25 \\ 0\cdot50 & 1\cdot125 & 1\cdot125 & 0\cdot75 & 0\cdot875 \\ 0\cdot25 & 0\cdot25 & 0\cdot25 & 0\cdot875 & 0\cdot25 \end{matrix}$$

Σ 3·25   3·375   3·375   4·375   1·875

The severe flaws in this tool have been identified by italicised words in the explanatory text. The first flaw has been discussed by Werner[13] and Alao.[14] Not all networks have a solution matrix. It is clear that when more than one independent sub-network exists no solution matrix can exist, but even within an integrated network there will only necessarily be a solution matrix when certain conditions are met. This point was first raised by Werner and the conditions have been specified formally by Alao. The second objection is that even where a solution network exists it may have a value of n much greater than the diameter of the network, and thus include an unspecified amount of redundant cycling. A solution to this is to define the *shortest path matrix* as the lowest power of the connectivity matrix for which all cells in the T_n matrix have positive values.[15] Such a matrix does not however have the mathematical properties of a solution matrix *sensu strictu*.

Although these first definitions appear to be shaky, attempts have been made to develop the tool without changing the definitional basis. The first consists of a revised powering procedure

$$a^n T_n = a^1 C^1 + a^2 C^2 + a^3 C^3 + \ldots + a^n C^n \qquad (4.8)$$

in which a is a positive scalar of less than one (the Katz[17] scalar). The process of squaring the scalar diminishes the value of each term; for example if $a = 0 \cdot 5$

$$a^n T_n = 0 \cdot 5 C^1 + 0 \cdot 25 C^2 + 0 \cdot 125 C^3 + \ldots + 0 \cdot 5^n C^n \qquad (4.9)$$

The row and column totals of the matrix can then be interpreted as before but it is clear that the accessibility of a node will be high when connections are direct and lower when connections are indirect.[16] The scalar matrix T_n (where $a = 0 \cdot 5$) is given for the connectivity matrix in table 4.3. A critical value in this analysis will be the value of this scalar. It may either be decided on a subjective basis, or as the best fit to parameters of a given data set.

The second application of the matrix is to use the powered values of C to construct shortest path matrices, $D_1, D_2, \ldots D_n$, (see table 4.3). The matrix D_n can then be interpreted as recording the highest level of connectivity between two nodes, the general accessibility of individual nodes, and thence the general accessibility of the network.[18] The general accessibility of the individual node is given by the Shimbel index

$$S(i) = \sum_{j=1}^{n} d_{ij} \qquad (4.10)$$

The mean and variance of the S values of all vertices in the matrix can then be used as measures of accessibility in the network as a whole.

This index was tested by Werner for the eight networks discussed in a preceding section. He concluded that the mean and the variance of the S values for individual nodes did discriminate between all eight networks. In addition the index suggested that networks C, D and E exhibited increasing accessibility, but decreasing uniformity of accessibility, a point illustrated by values in table 4.4. There was

TABLE 4.4

THE MEANS AND VARIANCES OF THE SHIMBEL INDEX
APPLIED TO EIGHT IDEAL NETWORKS

Network	*Shimbel index*	
(see figure 4.5)	*mean*	*Variance*
A	83·5	134·7
B	65·3	51·5
C	80·0	140·0
D	63·4	84·4
E	61·4	83·4
F	68·2	166·8
G	64·2	98·9
H	58·9	71·7

Source: Werner, *op. cit.*, p. 139, table 2.

no evidence that the index could distinguish the directional bias or the radial-circular distinctions evident in the geometry of the three networks.[19]

Finally it is possible to measure the dispersion of a network

$$D = \sum_{i=1}^{n} \cdot \sum_{j=1}^{n} d_{ij} \qquad (4.11)$$

and from this the mean and variance of d_{ij} in a network. Although it is clear that D, the mean of d_{ij} and the mean of S are linearly related, the variances may reveal different aspects of accessibility within the network. It is for example possible to have a high variance for d_{ij} (journeys vary greatly in complexity) when the variance of S values is zero (all vertices are equally well connected).

Factor Analysis of Abstract Graphs

In a study of Venezuela's airline network Garrison and Marble have used factor analysis of the connectivity latent structure within the system[20] (chapter 7, below). The same method in essence was applied by Gould to road networks, but the results are not altogether satisfactory.[21] Tinkler has returned to the problem with rather greater success.[22] He concludes that the most elegant method is to employ the principal eigenvector of the original connectivity matrix. He interprets this eigenvector 'in part as a measure of the differentiation of the nodes in the network and in part as a measure of the total integration of the network'.[23]

An obvious objection to the matrix methods, however they are developed, is the inflexibility of the binary format. One answer to this may well lie in the method employed by Gauthier.[24] He rejected the binary assumption and suggested that all connections could be weighted for such characteristics as length, route quality and move-ment costs. He constructed a connectivity matrix for São Paulo State in which non-zero elements were estimated according to distance and type of road. The resulting connectivity matrix is susceptible to many of the manipulations already discussed. Although such weighting may introduce a subjective element, it brings the analysis into closer line with the operating characteristics of the network.

4.3 TRANSPORT NETWORKS AS RADIAL STRUCTURES

Tinkler has suggested a rather different topological approach which has not yet been widely applied.[25] He first considers all networks as radial structures around a central pole and demonstrates that such structures obey a number of simple rules. Given a primary pole P the parameters can be defined: the *topological radius* of the net r_{max} (that is, the number of edges in the shortest path between the primary pole and the remotest vertex); an *incremental term* c (which governs the number of additional nodes on the ith radius to the number at the $(i - 1)$th radius); N_{rmax}, the *number of vertices in the network;* and the *nodality* of a vertex, being the number of edges incident at that vertex.

Empirical work suggests that most geographical networks can be fitted to these parameters by plotting the frequency distributions of nodes for all r values and comparing these frequency distributions with those of ideal nets. Tinkler concludes that in most cases the ap-propriate ideal network is a special case which he calls the *partially connected snowflake network*. For such networks it is possible, given c, to predict the nodality of the system and of parts of the system, and to compare these results with reality. He also demonstrates that the structures have implications for flow in the network. Tinkler's work is obviously of potential importance but two fundamental doubts already exist. The first concerns the assumption that nets can be considered as radial structures and that a nodal point (*P*) can be unequivocally identified; Tinkler does not demonstrate that the results will be independent of the choice of *P*. Secondly it must be noted that the mathematical model is deterministic and that there is no satisfactory method of testing the significance of deviations from the ideal structures.

Although the topological approach has introduced greater mathematical rigour into studies of network form it is far from clear that the results to date represent a step forward. The problems lie in three fields: the simplification of networks prior to analysis, the lack of independence in the indices and the interpretation of the results. Although progress has been made on all three fronts the problems have not yet been overcome.

5 The Explanation of Network Form

The observed variations in network characteristics demand explanation. In this discussion it is possible to identify two types of explanation and two levels of aggregation. The two types of explanation can be characterised as idiographic (or historical) and nomothetic (or law-making). The two levels of aggregation are the network element (an individual route or access point) and the network as a whole. Although the historical approach is most commonly applied to network elements and the nomothetic approach to whole networks, there is no necessary relation between the level of aggregation and the type of explanation advanced.

5.1 NETWORK ELEMENTS

The alignment of an individual route or the location of an access point such as a port or an airport becomes the first problem of network morphology. In explaining route locations O'Dell[1] and Appleton[2] identify the importance of landforms, geological structure, drainage pattern and other factors of the natural landscape. These constituted an initial transport surface on which some routes were evidently more attractive than others. Similarly Bird, and others, have identified those coastal landforms which encourage or impede port development.[3] Although such studies throw considerable light on individual cases (and may provide the basis for a typology of network elements —for example, Bird's 'anyport' and Appleton's 'valley routeways'), they do not have a great explanatory insight into the general processes of network development.

The Historical Explanation applied to Network Elements

An important aspect of such studies is to identify the demand for a transport facility. In many cases routes have been built to serve a specific productive activity. For example the Peak Forest Canal was first built to carry the limestone from the Derbyshire Peak district to the Manchester conurbation via the Ashton canal.[4] Similarly O'Connor has studied East African railway lines which were primarily built to handle mineral traffic.[5] In other cases, notably the great shipping canals, construction was undertaken to facilitate a traffic which was already well established.[6] In studying such historical data it is important to note that the most publicised 'reason' for construction was not necessarily the most important to the effective decision makers, and that the demand for a facility may change during its construction or subsequent life. This is especially true of many early routes—rail, canal or road—which were later to become segments of much larger systems, so that their original local purpose has been replaced by a national or even international function.

In interpreting the past demand for transport networks care must be taken to avoid anachronism. Thus the railway systems of the United States and Canada were built to open up new territory—they were not intended to serve the great urban centres which have since developed. The difficulties inherent in the correct reconstruction of past transport situations have been elegantly outlined by Vance in his study of the Union Pacific Railroad and the Oregon Trail. The pioneers of both trail and railroad chose similar routes, but whereas the trail was based upon 'water and the almost unbroken line of grassland' (that is, the needs of livestock) and 'terrain seems to have played only an indirect role', the railroad took 'the line of least wasted effort... not the least summits... [but]... minimum redundant grade'.[7] The locations coincided; their determinants were very different.

The emphasis on the original demand for transportation as it was seen by the pioneers is a theme of Meinig's work.[8] He argued that the number of routes chosen fell far below the number proposed (this has been demonstrated in a number of research contexts); therefore the identification of proximate causes is only possible in the study of boardroom minutes and similar documents. Dyos has pointed out another complexity, that the motives of past route builders and their allies might themselves be mixed. He suggests that in Victorian London at least, 'the ideas of most of the improvers, of the champions of the poor, and of the railway promoters temporarily complemented each other'; and railway building and slum clearance became twin motives in track alignment through the London suburbs.[9]

It can be observed that in many cases political boundaries gave
rise to distinctive patterns of network. Three such effects can be
identified: the duplication of facilities, the lack of connection between
facilities and the distortion of network form. All three effects are
evident in the railway networks on the US–Canadian border, a pattern
first identified by Jones[10] (figure 5.1). The duplication of facilities

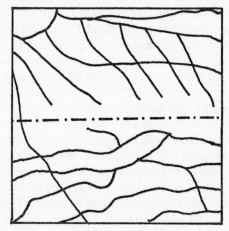

*Fig. 5.1. Rail networks on the border between Canada
and the United States*

also occurs with pipelines, as in the Middle East, and with canals.
Sealy points out that the closeness of international boundaries in
north-west Europe has resulted in an 'excessive' number of international airports in the London–Paris–Brussels–Amsterdam area.[11]
The lack of connection between facilities may take the form of
distinct breaks in the network[12] or a more subtle form such as
breaks in railway gauge.[13]

Finally, as Appleton noted, 'Many features of the present pattern
arise from the fact that they came into existence against a background
of competition'.[14] Competition of this type occurred in the building
of ports, canals, turnpike roads and railways, although in some
cases, as for example at the height of the railway era, there were
attempts at government control to prevent the wasteful duplication
of capacity. Appleton instances the Leen valley in Nottinghamshire
as an example of such duplication. There three lines were built by

three separate companies—the Midland Railway building a branch line from Nottingham to Mansfield, the Manchester, Sheffield and Lincolnshire Railway building a new trunk route to London, and the Great Northern seeking only the coal traffic of the Derbyshire–Nottingham coalfield. At a quite different scale one can recognise that competition led to the construction of no less than six routes between Chicago and Omaha.[15]

Nomothetic Approaches to the Optimal Location of Network Elements

These empirical approaches can be complemented by the theoretical consideration of route and access point location. Many of these ideas were derived in the practice of transport planning, and as such tend to identify optimal route patterns. Although elements of optimising behaviour must be considered, they cannot be treated as the sole determinants of route morphology.

Positive and negative deviations were identified by Wellington, who was an engineer engaged in construction of the railway between Vera Cruz and Mexico City in the 1880s. This project provided the stimulus for his thinking in an *Economic Theory for the Location of Railways*.[16] Wellington assumed that the origin and destination of the route were known. His concern was to provide a rationale for deviation from the direct route. He identified those deviations which were designed to maximise traffic, termed by Haggett positive deviations. The range of possibilities lies between minimum distance (figure 5.2a) and maximum traffic (figure 5.2b). Haggett also identifies an intermediate solution which is optimal, granted certain assumptions about traffic, revenue and traffic 'lost' at theose centres which are not directly served.[17] The most common example of this positive deviation today can be seen in airline operations.

Negative deviation is the avoidance of an obstacle. In most cases these obstacles are features of physical geography and route builders will wish to avoid the high costs of construction which the obstacle involves (figure 5.2c). It may also be a feature of economic or social geography—high value agricultural land, valuable urban land and areas protected by conservation policies may all result in deviations from a direct route. In most cases where the barrier is a natural feature the deflecting effect can be considered in terms of construction costs. In the other cases the decision may be based more on the political

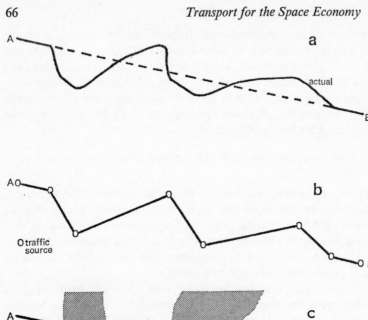

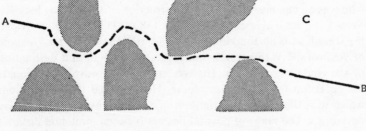

Fig. 5.2. Negative and positive deviations in route alignment

strength of the objectors than on any explicit cost calculation. This can be illustrated by a number of motorway location disputes in Great Britain during the 1960s.

A similar argument was adopted by Losch.[18] He considered the problem of selecting the cheapest route between two points which lie in regions with different but internally homogeneous transport costs. The problem also raises the question of port location, as the optimal route will also identify, *ceteris paribus*, the optimal trans-shipment point location. Losch claimed that the least cost route could be identified by using the sine law. The simple example in the diagram (figure 5.3) identifies two regions A and B with transport costs f_a and f_b respectively. The least cost route is identified as being one in which the ratio of the *sines* of the angles α and β should equal the ratio of the costs f_a and f_b. (This solution is analogous to the law of refraction which describes the path taken by a ray of light moving from a dense into a less dense medium; the term *law of refraction*

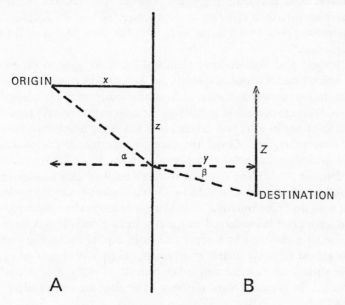

Fig. 5.3. The least cost route problem

is therefore sometimes used to refer to the transport analogue.) The number of possible locations satisfying this condition is large. The unique solution[19] is given by the equation for total costs

$$T = f_a(x^2 + z^2)^{\frac{1}{2}} + f_b(y^2 + (Z - z)^2)^{\frac{1}{2}} \qquad (5.1)$$

This can be simplified and differentiated to yield minimum total costs, when

$$0 = 0 \cdot 5 f_a (x^2 + z^2)^{-\frac{1}{2}} (2z) + 0 \cdot 5 f_b (y^2 + Z^2 + z^2 - 2Zz)^{-\frac{1}{2}} (2z - 2Z) \qquad (5.2)$$

The equation can then be solved for z given f_a, f_b, x, y and Z.

Losch illustrates this argument by reference to routes between east and west coasts of North America. Before construction of the Panama canal three routes were available: sea (via Cape Horn), sea and land (across the isthmus) and land. The construction of a canal across the isthmus could also be seen as an application of this law, with a choice of location in part determined by the relative costs of sea mileage and canal mileage. The same principle of re-fraction also plays an important role in the relation between transport nets with different cost structures and in the location of interchange points such as railways. This has been demonstrated by Domanski.[20]

Bunge[21] and Werner have identified the more general problem, of which Losch's is only a special case, as being the selection of least cost routes across surfaces with continuously varying transport costs. Werner succeeds in identifying the minimum cost path between two locations in a 'region divided into any finite number of homo-geneous subregions. Given the per ton mile transportation costs and assuming that total transportation costs are a linear function of distance . . . '.[22] The limits to Werner's solution may be identified as follows: firstly it does not deal with a continuously varying surface, but with an approximation of numerous homogeneous subregions; and secondly it is concerned with a cost surface only. It may be able to model a surface which represents both capital and social costs; it is almost certainly unable to represent the equally important vari-able surface of revenue and other benefits. Thirdly it is doubtful whether, in general, costs within a subregion are independent of direction.

Reference has already been made to the relevance of the law of refraction to the location of ports and railway stations. It is clear however that the analysis should be extended to include variations in construction and operating costs between locations. In the case of airport location a number of excellent analyses by Sealy[23] have been followed by the Roskill Commission on the siting of a third London airport.[24] This study not only identified the categories of data which should be considered but proposed a methodology by which they were integrated in projections of traffic, costs and benefits. Although the logic of this analysis has been shown to produce curious results *reductio and absurdum*, it pointed to the type of analysis which can be employed[25]. Only a few studies have been addressed to the question whether existing airports are in any sense optimally located.[26] A full summary of the considerations in port location appraisal is given by bird.[27]

Even when a particular transport system has a long history it can be argued that the contemporary pattern of facilities is the result

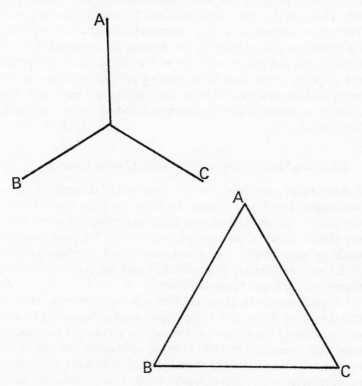

Fig. 5.4. Two 'optimal' networks

of competitive selection over time. (For example, the present ports of the United Kingdom are the survivors of a much greater number which existed in the Middle Ages.) The process of competitive selection is based in part on the ability of a facility to attract traffic and therefore funds for expansion. Although it can be doubted whether such a process tends towards an optimum location, it can clearly lead to the elimination of the most ill-judged locations.[28]

In contemporary decisions the analysis of costs and benefits is explicit, and their true complexity has been identified in many studies of transport planning. One key element in such studies is the specification of the quantity to be maximised or minimised and the accounting time period. The importance of the former point is illustrated in figure 5.4 where both networks are 'optimal': the first minimises the construction costs and the second the user costs.[29] The relation of these two to give minimum total cost will be dependent on additional information on the demand for transportation, the interest rates and the economic life of the project. These distinctions are of prime importance when defining optimal locations, and as many modern networks are being designed in accordance with these criteria their relevance to explanation must necessarily be of increasing importance.

Behavioural Interpretations of Network Element Location

It is clear that some routes do not come within the assumptions of Wellington, Losch and Werner. In many cases the origin but not the destination was known, and there was initial ignorance about the characteristics of the region through which the route was later made to pass. Gould argues that, in colonial countries at least, routes were exploratory in nature, and that the correct analogy is therefore to be found in search theory.[30]

The problem can be illustrated from a hypothetical case. Suppose that the colony is first settled at a seaport marked X, and exploration on foot allows an assessment of territory for a radius of y kilometres only. This assessment includes both the difficulty of the terrain and the potential benefits of the route (whether in revenue, agricultural production or some administrative goal). The construction of an optimum first leg is therefore authorised in the light of this knowledge (figure 5.5). In the second time period there is a choice between the second best route in the original zone of information (such as route 2a) or the best route in the new field of information (route 2b). But at this stage the element of pure comparison has an element of risk also, for route 2a will lead to a lesser increase in information than the adventurous 2b. On the other hand the less adventurous choice may also be safer—for discoveries may be welcome or unwelcome. Throughout the development process there will therefore be a sequence of choices between speculative route construction and consolidation in areas already served by an incomplete network.

Similar elements of game theory can be detected in the competitive relations between route builders. This branch of social theory was originally devised by von Neumann and Morgenstern to analyse situations in which some *constants* are known, some variables are known within a given *probability*, and some are completely *unknown*.[31]

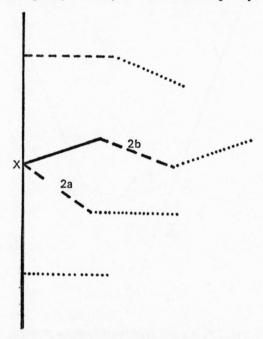

Fig. 5.5. An exploratory route building sequence

For example, in a child's game of chance the number of squares on the board is known, the probability of any given dice score can be predicted, but the behaviour of the opponent, initially at least, may be entirely unknown.

Consider for example the case in figure 5.6. Two railway companies (I and II) have reached points A and B on the way to C. The only traffic (towards C) to offer revenue in the intervening region is located at X and would yield revenue R_x to the carrier. There are four possible routes through the intervening region, two of which are

direct and two of which serve X at an additional track mileage
which is expressed as an annual cost of C_2 and C_3 respectively. If
neither railway serves X the traffic will go to point Z on railway
I's route 1. If both railways serve X it is assumed that the traffic
will be shared equally between them. The possibilities of the situation

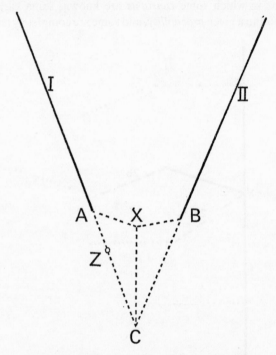

Fig. 5.6. A game type route location problem

are outlined in table 5.1, which represents the results to the companies
of all possible combinations of routes, and is termed a pay-off
table.

The management of railway I has a choice between routes 1 and
2. Inspection of the table shows that if company I chooses location
1 it will either gain all R or gain nothing. If on the other hand it
chooses location 2 it is certain to make at least $\frac{1}{2}R_x - C_2$ but never
more than $R_x - C_2$. It is also noteworthy that this safest choice
precludes the optimum solution for the whole railway system, which

is routes 1 and 4. It may be objected that railway II is certain to choose route 3 and there is therefore no uncertainty affecting I's decision, but this is not necessarily so. Suppose that commercial intelligence is such that railway I does not know whether the value of $\frac{1}{2}R_x - C_3$ is positive; then II's decision is unpredictable, and I is forced to decide in the game theory context.

TABLE 5.1

PAY-OFF TABLE FOR THE ROUTE LOCATION GAME
IN FIGURE 5.6

Route choices made		Results		Net returns to system		Status of
I Railway	II	I	II	Value	Rank	I's strategy
1	3	0	$R - C_3$	$R_x - C_3$	joint 2nd	
						Maximum risk
1	4	R_x	0	R_x	best	
2	3	$\frac{1}{2}R_x - C_2$	$\frac{1}{2}R_x - C_3$	$R_x - C_2 - C_3$	worst	
						Maximum guaranteed return
2	4	$R_x - C_2$	0	$R_x - C_2$	joint 2nd	

TABLE 5.2

RAILWAY LOCATION GAME: PAY-OFF TABLE
FOR RAILWAY I WHEN ALLOWING II TO ACT FIRST

Route choice by II	Best reply by I	Pay-off to I
3	2	$\frac{1}{2}R_x - C_2$
4	1	R_x

The game can also be extended to consider a question which may well arise in the boardroom of railway I: 'shall we act first, or rather wait until II has shown its hand?' Under the pay-off as established in table 5.1 the decision is clearly to wait. If II acts first then I can respond as in table 5.2 and ensure a minimum gain of $\frac{1}{2}R_x - C_2$ and a maximum of R_x.

If however the proportion of R is not fifty–fifty but three to one in favour of the first comer, a revised version of the tables yields three courses of action for railway I (table 5.3). Inspection of these reveals that to build route 1 first is an inferior strategy to waiting, as long as $\frac{1}{4}R_x$ is greater than C_2. The least risky strategy is to build 2 first, and ensure a minimum result of $\frac{3}{4}R_x - C_2$ (assuming that this too is positive) (table 5.4).

TABLE 5.3

RAILWAY LOCATION GAME:
RANGE OF STRATEGIES AVAILABLE TO RAILWAY I

Timing by I	Decision I	II	Pay-off to I Value	Rank	Comments to I
Act first	1 → 3		0	joint 7th	Maximum
	1 → 4		R	joint 1st	risk
	2 → 3		$\frac{3}{4}R_x - C_2$	5th	Minimum
	2 → 4		$R_x - C_2$	joint 3rd	risk
Wait	1 ← 3		0	joint 7th	—
	2 ← 3		$\frac{1}{4}R_x - C_2$	6th	Best reply
	1 ← 4		R_x	joint 1st	Best reply
	2 ← 4		$R_x - C_2$	joint 3rd	—

Arrows indicate time sequence

A similar analysis can be applied to the location of access points. Consider two ports competing for a common hinterland and both planning a major increase in capacity. The timing of this investment has to consider two factors: the expected increase in demand and the behaviour of the competitor. The longer construction is delayed the

TABLE 5.4

SUMMARY OF STRATEGIES FOR RAILWAY I

Summary:	Build 1	0	or	R_x
	2	$\frac{3}{4}R_x - C_2$	or	$R_x - C$
	Wait—			
	best reply	$\frac{1}{4}R_x - C_2$	or	R_x

higher will be the initial traffic, and therefore returns, but the chance of being forestalled by the competitor is similarly increased. Isard considers a similar situation in which there are two cities considering airport development and defines the conditions under which they might agree to share a single intermediate location with distribution of revenue.[32] On the other hand recent changes in attitude to airport noise suggest that there may be groups anxious to avoid the location of an airport in their area. The problem therefore falls into the field explored by Wolpert.[33]

It cannot be claimed that the explanation of network element locations is satisfactory. The historical approaches can claim factual accuracy, and in the hands of skilled scholars have produced valuable insights. They do not, and some would argue can never, lead to a general statement. Attempts which have been made to derive such general statements inductively are marked by their banality. On the other hand the theoretical approaches are so narrowly constrained that their application, except in a broadly interpretative sense, is severely limited. It may be that the explanatory problem is incapable of solution at this level of aggregation, and that the answer is found in the configuration not of individual elements but of whole networks.

5.2 THE STRUCTURE OF NETWORKS

An association has long been recognised between network density and economic development on an international scale. Owen uses evidence of this association to support his claim that transport investment is a prerequisite of economic development. Haggett discusses the association between network density (road and rail) and the degree of economic development as measured by Berry's technological and demographic indices. He concluded that the association appeared strongest for rail networks. Anomalies in the result were explicable either in idiographic terms (for example his historical interpretation of the dense network in Taiwan) or in data problems (for example the uneven distribution of both route networks and development in such countries as Canada and Australia). A further point made by Haggett is that 'the lack of correspondence between the low values on the two media suggests that railways have served as a substitute for roads'.[34] Such a complementarity of the two modes may reflect geographical conditions within the countries concerned or differences in the historical period of development.

Rigorous Empirical Analysis

A more comprehensive investigation of such associations is made by Kansky.[35] He employed a variety of measures of network density and form and analysed their geographical correlates in two stages. In an exploratory phase a sample of twenty-five countries was selected. For each of these countries he calculated two indices of railway network form, two indices of road network form, two of economic development and one each for size, shape and relief of the country. This data was subjected to regression analysis. Kansky concluded

More developed countries tend to have shorter edge length and a higher number of high order intersections and *vice versa*. Demographic structure had little influence . . . size is of some importance especially for highway networks, the greater the size of country the greater the average edge length, and the less the number of high order intersections. Shape is of no significance . . . relief has a significant influence upon railroad networks: countries with variable relief tend to have longer average rail edge length.[36]

On the basis of these results Kansky investigated three further topics. The first was the use of other measures of economic development as an independent variable: this proved an unfruitful line of enquiry. The second was to compare the measures of network form with each other by correlation analysis: no correlation coefficient approached 1·00 and it could therefore be assumed that none of the network measures was redundant. Finally he examined the pattern of residuals from regression and concluded that high residuals were common in those countries which had networks strongly linked to neighbouring countries. An attempt to revise the network measures to incorporate this feature was not successful.[37]

The use of regression analysis was also adopted by Taaffe, Morrill and Gould[38] to investigate the distribution of highway density in Nigeria and Ghana. They demonstrated that highway mileage in administrative units could be related to the population and area of the unit. The best fit linear regression used the logarithms of the independent variables and explained 75 per cent and 81 per cent of the observed variation in Ghana and Nigeria respectively. The authors then mapped the pattern of residuals from regression and associated them in qualitative terms with 'hostile environment', rail competition, interregional highways and commercialisation of agriculture.[39] Kansky also used his indices in an attempt to explain intra-national variations in network form in the United States. In this case his independent socio-economic variables were sales *per caput* and electric energy consumption *per caput*. He again considered relief, size and shape. Once again some associations were identified but no strong pattern of association emerged.[40]

Finally note can be taken of attempts to examine the spatial correlates of network density within urban areas. Here a high degree of connectivity and low edge length can be assumed. Borchert in his study of Minneapolis–St Paul related route density to distance from the city centre, the period of development and the size of landholding plots. The strongest association was with this last variable.[41]

The inconclusive nature of these studies (in terms of significance levels), and problems of interpreting the observed spatial correlations, highlight the need for a stronger theoretical basis. In Kansky's work, for example, there is no clear distinction between correlates which are surrogates for demand and those which are surrogates for supply; furthermore there are some 'independent' variables which might equally be considered as results, not as determinants of network construction.

Attempts to Construct a General Theory

Attempts have been made to tie these disparate findings into a more general theory of network structure and to represent that theory in a testable form. These attempts fall into two groups which may be characterised as cross-sectional and evolutionary. In the cross-sectional approach the network at a given point in time is 'explained' by independent variables at that same period. In the evolutionary approach the development of the network through time is explained reference to a number of changing independent variables.

The best example of the cross-section approach appears in the final chapter of Kansky's study.[42] He used his empirical studies to derive a set of nine propositions or axioms and a set of predictive equations. This semi-axiomatic system was then used to predict the form of the Sicilian railway network in 1908. The first stage was to use the equations to predict the expected number of vertices, the expected number of edges, the expected β index and the expected η index. By implication this also predicts network length ($e.\eta$) and hence density. The second stage was to devise a simulation procedure. Thirty main urban settlements were selected and the probability that each would be served by the network was set directly proportional to the total estimated income of the settlement. This probability field was used to select the expected number of vertices (a high

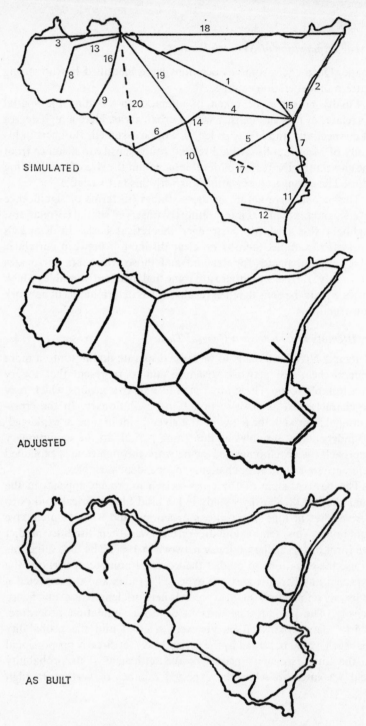

Fig. 5.7. The results of a network simulation (after Kansky)

estimate of 18 and a low estimate of 15). The vertices thus selected were connected by edges according to the rule

connect the two largest centres of economic activity; gradually add edges in such a way that the next centre joins the largest and closest centre which is already located on the network. After all selected vertices are located on the network and edges remain to be allocated, the same rule may be used again, in a slightly different form . . . add the edge in such a way that the circuit between the first, second and third largest centres is completed.[43]

There was also a supplementary rule to eliminate direct duplication of routes. This was employed again in the second stage of the simulation in which further simplification was adopted to reduce mean edge length in accordance with prediction wherever the configuration of the country allowed the merging of parallel routes. The stages of the simulation and its apparent success can be appreciated visually in figure 5.7.

A parallel type of simulation was employed by Kolars and Malin in their study of Turkey.[44] In that simulation the independent variable was a specially constructed population potential map. The probability of a link between urban centres was made directly proportional to the product of their population and inversely proportional to distance between them. The resulting network was then adjusted for parsimony of route lengths and the completion of circuits, the latter on the specious grounds that dead-end routes would be inefficient in practice, and the addition of links to ensure alternative routes to all places. Again the simulation was visually effective.

An immediate problem in both these studies is the definition of independent and dependent variables. In Kansky's study the socio-economic data referred to 1908, not to the periods of route construction. The Turkish study, astonishingly, used population in 1964 to simulate a railway system which had been constructed many years before. Such anachronism seems doubly dangerous if it is noted that the establishment of a route system may itself be the cause of population concentration at certain nodes.

A careful use of the evolutionary approach will acknowledge this interdependence of the relevant variables by modelling their interaction in space through time, in a sequenced prediction of the transport network. Such a sequence is proposed by Taaffe and his associates in their study of West African transport networks.[45]

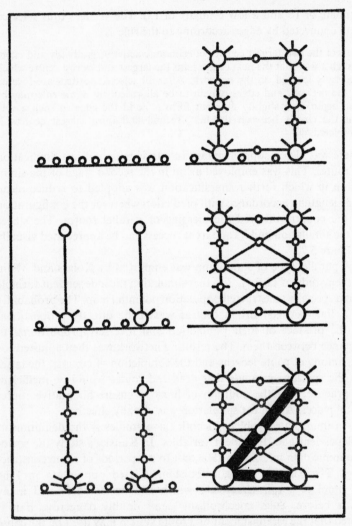

Fig. 5.8. The sequence of network development
(after Taaffe, Morrill and Gould)

Once again the ideas were derived from extensive empirical work, already referred to, and the authors are careful to term their construct an 'ideal-typical' sequence, but it has since been widely adopted as if it had much greater explanatory power. The six phases of the sequence are illustrated in figure 5.8. The sequence as a whole seems to the present author to have two serious flaws. Firstly, it is so closely related to the historical developments in Nigeria and Ghana that its application in other areas will do little more than demonstrate how like (or unlike) that network is to those of anglophone West Africa. (Burghardt, who investigated its relevance to the Niagara peninsula, concluded that the sequence observed was different in the North American context,[46] while examination of the contiguous West African states suggests that there too a different pattern evolved.) Secondly, the sequence appears to have strong geometric symmetry but no internal logic. Finally it should be noted that the theory is concerned primarily with connectivity while the accompanying empirical study is concerned with density. Despite these objections the sequence of port development posited by this scheme has attracted the attention of several authors. Rimmer develops the logic of port competition and elimination with special reference to the Australasian experience.[47] Ogundana has examined its application to Nigerian port development in greater depth and introduces the concept of 'port diffusion' into parts of the coastline whose port potential was previously undeveloped.[48]

A similar type of sequence has been derived in theoretical terms by Lachene.[49] His study starts from an assumed inland plain with local transport links between the smallest initial settlements, and the development of important centres and routes is seen as an endogenous process. It is obvious that this type of approach is convergent upon the traditional analyses of location theory and their recent elaboration.[50] It is perhaps for this reason that the most satisfactory attempt at the simulation of a transport network is the work done by Morrill in central Sweden.[51] His interest lay not in the transport network alone but in the whole social and economic geography of a relatively small region. The simulation was based on Monte Carlo techniques with five distinct stages in the prediction of the socio-economic landscape between 1860 and 1960. The probability of a particular route being built in a given time period was based upon 'the distance of the routes, population, especially urban of the areas traversed, and the costs of construction . . . . It may be observed that the location of assigned cities or railways often coincided with the actual location'.[52]

At this stage Morrill acknowledges the profound problems of

theory building and testing in this field. The first concerns axioms or rules of simulation. Kansky admitted that many of his nine propositions did not qualify as axioms *sensu strictu*.[53] Attention has already been drawn to the rather curious rules employed by Kolars and Malin. In the study by Taaffe, Morrill and Gould the 'rules' of network development have no logical status whatsoever. Even in the stronger study by Kansky the rules were only operational when used with empirically derived predictive equations. The second problem concerns conventions for testing of simulation, whether cross-sectional or evolutionary. As Moore and Brown have argued, the problem is not whether the simulated pattern has properties which seem visually similar to those of reality, but whether the observed pattern could 'reasonably be said to have been drawn from a multidimensional frequency distribution... generated by *n* runs of the simulation', and 'relatively little progress has been made towards the establishment of such a test'.[54] But even if such a test can be defined or if the network is clearly identical with the result of simulation, the problem remains, for radically different processes may yet produce convergent forms. A simulation system may produce perfect replicas of reality, but yet be totally erroneous in the axioms by which it interprets the decision-making processes of reality. It is this conclusion which reasserts the complementarity at this stage of historical and nomothetic approaches.

6 Technical and Economic Properties of Transport Networks

The consideration of abstract geometrical properties of networks must not exclude the study of technical and economic properties. Such properties have been widely studied by engineers and economists but rarely by geographers, with the exception of a few scholars such as O'Dell[1] and Ullman[2] and a few topics such as railway gauges.[3] In the present analysis these properties are important for two reasons: the extent to which they exhibit spatial variation, and the extent to which they give rise to spatial variation in other phenomena.

6.1 TECHNICAL PROPERTIES: CAPACITY

Three groups of technical properties can be considered: those which limit total traffic, those which limit the type of traffic and those which represent indivisibilities in the supply of capacity.

Limitations on the total capacity of a network may arise from the design of access points, junctions or routes. Limitation by access points is of great importance in air and sea transport, of lesser importance in rail transport, and of comparative unimportance in road transport where, in general, the total number of access points is extremely high. Junctions are of critical importance in rail and road networks, often imposing capacity constraints far beyond their geographical location. The point is succinctly made by Garrison and Marble with reference to the networks in figure 6.1.

Technically a cut (or bottleneck) is a collection of directed routes and intersections through which passes every route from source to destination. . . [in figure 6.1a] clearly the maximum flow from the source to the destination cannot be greater than the capacity of the node marked with an asterisk. In a complicated network [figure 6.1b] . . . it is by no means immediately apparent what the flow capacity of the network is, nor where the minimum cut lies.[4]

Limitation by route capacity is generally confined to road, canal and rail networks, but there are occasions when air or sea space becomes so crowded that, with a given safety factor, the effective limit has been reached.

The question of indivisibilities occurs in the provision of all network capacity, but is of varying importance. In road transport

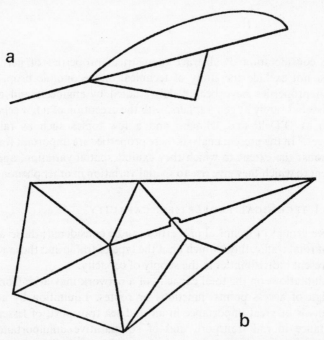

Fig. 6.1. The max-flow min-cut problem (after Garrison and Marble)

the network can be supplied initially in very elementary form and extended and improved as traffic increases. Railways, on the other hand, suffer greatly from indivisibilities in the provision of track. The problem not only differs as between modes but may also vary from time to time and from place to place. In most transport technologies the minimum size of unit has increased. Thus in port construction the unit of investment is usually a berth, with a capacity upwards of 100 000 tons per annum. In a few cases the indivisibilities are imposed by the site conditions. For example the Portbury port development project near Bristol was dependent upon investment in tide gates to control water levels at the quays. The costs of this structure implied a minimum investment in nine new berths, a major increment of capacity.[5]

Rail Networks

In the study of rail networks two statistics are critical determinants of route capacity: maximum train size and the number of train paths. Maximum train size is often determined by the initial strength of construction of rail, ballast and bridges. A further constraint is the ruling grade of the track (gradients), although this may be of reduced importance if more powerful engine units become available. Finally it can be noted that the length of tracks in marshalling yards or in passing loops may be a limit to train length and thus to train size. R. N. Taaffe has demonstrated that this was a major constraint on rail capacity in Soviet Central Asia.[6]

The number of train paths along a route is determined by route capacity, the number of tracks, junction capacity, the number of passing loops and the signalling technology available. In the simplest systems a single line is divided into 'blocks'; between the blocks are passing loops. Access to a block is controlled by a staff, or key, which controls the points at both ends of the block. The train entering the block carries the staff to the end of the block where it then becomes available for a reverse movement. Clearly this system cannot work easily unless the traffic is balanced. It is evident that this staff function can be replaced by an electronic device in automatic signalling systems, but the block principle is retained. It will also be evident that the number of train paths in each direction is partly dependent upon the scheduling of traffic. If movements are homogeneous with regard to speed, passing loops will only be utilised for oncoming traffic, but if average speeds are heterogeneous the loops must also be available for overtaking. These problems are least on multiple track lines, but much of the world's railway network is single track, and long stretches of more than double track are extremely rare.[7] Joy has suggested that even small amounts of multiple track on heavy traffic lines may be an undesirable luxury, and has demonstrated that careful timetabling can allow a maintenance of present traffic volumes despite a great reduction in the track mileage.[8] The twin expedients of centralised electronic signalling and programmed timetabling have therefore allowed many routes to carry traffic far in excess of original specifications. A disadvantageous by-product of such improvements may be a reduction in the flexibility of the system, resulting in wide-ranging delays if mishaps occur.

It is probable that most railway stations have an effective limit to the traffic they can handle. In some cases this is due to track layout and signalling systems in the immediate vicinity of the station. Features of this type have for long limited the traffic handled by one of London's main line terminals, St Pancras. On other occasions the limit lies in the station facilities themselves. In the case of freight the limits are siding length, stacking areas and mechanical handling plant.

Railway networks seldom limit the type of traffic which can be carried. The best known limitation, gauge width, affects rolling stock rather than traffic, as also do limitations on axle or wagon weights. A curious limitation of this kind became apparent in the United Kingdom in the 1960s. The adoption of international container standards for rail transport was prevented by the low bridge clearances where rail is crossed by road on many major routes. Such a problem could be solved only by the provision of specially built rolling stock. Another limitation on type of capacity will be the handling facilities installed at railway stations; where such capacity is specialised, for example grain elevators, the capacity limits differ according to commodity.

Indivisibilities in network provision are marked in rail transport. The initial investment and each subsequent increment of capacity are large. Suppose the first installation is a single track of standard gauge with a limited number of passing loops (although Mellor has noted the use of narrow gauge track as the initial investment[9]); the capacity of the single track is of the order of three quarters of a million tons per annum in each direction. It is, however, possible to increase this by perhaps 20 per cent with more passing loops and improved signalling. The next increment in capacity, double track, more than doubles track capacity. Indivisibilities are less marked for railway termini except perhaps where specialised handling facilities are installed.

Road Networks

The specification of road capacities has become a complex part of highway engineering, beyond the scope of this study. It is, however, possible to identify the critical relationships and variables which must be considered in assessing existing routes and designing new routes.

There is a complex relationship between vehicle densities, vehicle speeds and route capacity. In general vehicle speeds are heterogeneous, so that each vehicle tends to reduce the average speed of

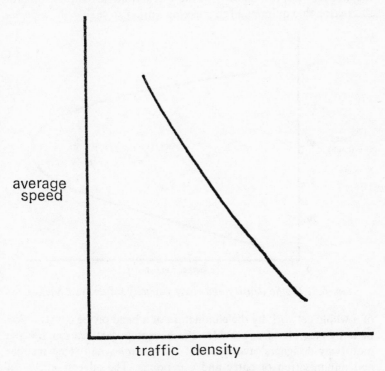

Fig. 6.2. Traffic speed and density

other vehicles. When densities are low this effect is minimal, but as traffic densities increase so the effect increases until all vehicles are moving at approximately the same speed; any further increase in density reduces speeds still further until at peak density (bumper-to-bumper) the flow becomes intermittent and average speeds are very low indeed. This pattern is suggested in figure 6.2. The capacity of the route, which can be defined as the product of speed and density, therefore increases until a certain density is reached (at a moderate speed) and then declines as speeds are reduced by congestion. An example of such a curve based on motorway data from Paris is given in figure 6.3.[10] Once a route has capacity traffic density, the maintenance of capacity speed is critical. If movements fall below capacity speed to negotiate a bend, to approach a junction or to pass slow moving vehicles, the capacity of the whole route is reduced. It is for this reason that quite small engineering works can change the capacity

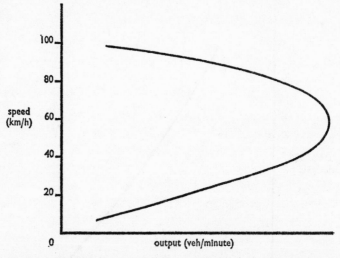

Fig. 6.3. Traffic density and route capacity (after Gerondeau)

of a whole network by the elimination of a bend or the construction of a by-pass. It also provides the economic justification for the motorway designers' avoidance of sharp curves and steep inclines and minimisation of entry and exit points. The adverse effects of slow moving or parked vehicles can also be avoided by posting of minimum speeds and prohibition of parking by the roadside.

It is important to note that capacity flow is not recognisable by the individual route user. For comfortable driving most road users prefer a route at a density very much below capacity, so that they can move at their own pace. On the other hand, even when capacity density is achieved some drivers, and indeed some slow-moving vehicles, will still seek to join the flow. This is because the benefits to them as individuals remain high while they need not, and do not, consider the penalties they impose on other users. It is clear that this is a critical aspect of the urban traffic problem.

Yet another concept of capacity may involve a consideration of costs. Suppose that there is a number of different road types—types of both construction and maintenance—for which the relation between traffic density and maintenance costs is known. The maximum capacity of a route may then be defined as the density (and therefore the implied speed and throughput) at which it becomes preferable to replace the route with one of higher density capacity. The graph in figure 6.4a is based on material collected by Soberman in Venezuela,[11] but it may well be that the curved relation (figure 6.4b) is more realistic, implying a steep increase in maintenance costs once a certain traffic density is exceeded. This is commonly asserted to occur in developing countries. The first road is a narrow earth road but as traffic increases it becomes more economic to tar first one lane and then two lanes. In Nigeria, for example, it was considered by Adedeji[12] that the critical densities are 50 vehicles per day for one-lane bitumen and 150 vehicles per day for two-lane bitumen, figures rather lower than those suggested by Soberman.[13]

Finally it is clear that a cost definition of capacity may be extended to total costs (not only maintenance costs) of network provision or total costs per unit of output (including operating costs). Such a calculation will evidently include many problems of definition, and certain problems are still to be resolved, such as the contribution of vehicles of various sizes to the wear and tear on the roadway which in turn affects operating costs.

Those responsible for road systems may find, under certain conditions, that it is necessary to impose restrictions on the type of vehicle capacity operated. In some cases these limits are purely a matter of safety, but in others they reflect the design strength of the roadway, its culverts and its bridges. The economies of large vehicle operation are marked, and for this reason trucking operators maintain a steady pressure for the removal or relaxation of restraints and for the increase in design specifications.[14] On the other hand limits on the length of vehicles are usually based on questions of operating safety. In most networks the limits are constant thoughout, but in those areas where much of the necessary regulation depends on sub-national authorities local variations can occur, as for example between states in the USA.

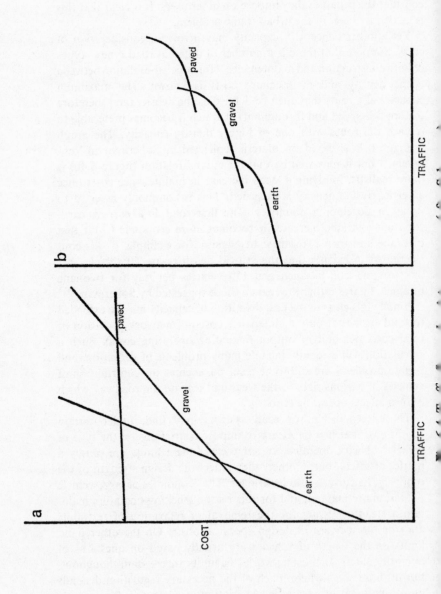

Airport Capacity

The limits to airport capacity are the subject of repeated re-evaluation in the light of technological change, and of considerable disagreement among those who are best informed. This disagreement can in part be attributed to subjective aspects of the assessment on questions of safety and environmental quality.

In technical terms the severest limits to capacity are limits of air space. The speed of airliners makes it necessary to ensure considerable spacing, vertical and lateral, of aircraft. The vagaries of air navigation make it impossible to ensure that all aircraft arrive in an airport's vicinity on strict schedule. As a result airports must have well defined approach paths and separate 'stacking' zones in which aircraft can circle while awaiting permission to land. Although these procedures have been facilitated by improved radar devices, automatic piloting and similar technological changes, other developments—notably aircraft speed, size and traffic growth—have prevented any spare capacity being available. It is this question of air space which places the severest limits on the capacity of individual airports and on their location in relation to each other.

Such already limited air space may be further reduced by other geographical features. In mountainous regions certain approach paths and air zones will be unsafe, either because of the altitude of the mountains or because of the meteorological effects such as turbulence to which they give rise. Further constraints may be imposed in the interests of environmental quality. There is well-justified suspicion that this consideration has been ignored in the past, but airport planners are becoming progressively more sensitive. An indication of the 'political' nature of this response is given by the index or noise exposure forecast employed in the United States. The NEF ranges from NEF_0, 'the contour beyond which reaction would be insignificant', and NEF_{25}, at which 'organised resistance might be expected'.[15] Similar indices have been employed in the United Kingdom, including NNI (noise and number index) and PNdB (perceived noise in decibels). It is clear that these problems will be acute in densely settled areas.

The capacity of a given airport in a particular time period may however be limited further by the runway space and navigational controls available. A French authority suggests that one runway can handle a minimum of 40 movements per hour,[16] but much higher figures (over 90) have been recorded. Twin parallel runways can increase capacity by a factor of two as long as the runways are sufficiently far apart to allow separate control of their approach paths. Finally it can be noted that the addition of cross runways does not ordinarily increase capacity but may allow continued operation in adverse weather. Once again there is a subjective element in estimates of capacity. The definition of acceptable safety limits may differ from the engineer to the airline operator, the pilot and the insurance companies involved.

Finally the capacity of an airport may be limited by the terminal facilities available. The introduction of 'jumbo jets' in the early 1970s increased the number of passengers that could be handled in terms of air space and runway space, but not in terms of terminal facilities. The increased flow of passengers threatened acute congestion in customs and immigration handling, baggage handling and in the handling of passengers on transport systems serving the airport. In the event no severe delays occurred but the presence of limits on capacity was clearly recognised.

Most airports will also have limits upon the size of aircraft which they can accept. The twin factors controlling this will be runway strength and runway length. Runway strength is seldom more than a temporary restriction on airport use which can be readily solved by reconstruction. Runway length on the other hand may be a permanent restriction. An airport built on a site restricted by landforms or by other land uses may be unable to make the necessary extensions, or if able, only at a cost which threatens the economic viability of the project. Such problems have been recurrent in airport planning in the United Kingdom, first with the 'inner' London airports and then with other airports such as Luton, Southend and Southampton. An elegant example of the problems of airport expansion and runway extension in Cyprus is given by Ody.[17] The problem has also been acute at coastal locations where runway extensions have on occasion utilised 'made-land' projecting into the sea.

The problems have increased in the period 1950–70 with rapid increases in both the weight of aircraft and the speed at which they take off and touch down. It is understood that if the supersonic airliner proposed by the United States were built it would require a runway exceeding 10 000 feet in length, and runways in excess of

7000 feet are standard equipment for major airports. On the other hand it has been strongly argued by technical experts that design improvements in the direction of short take-off or vertical take-off could render such runways obsolete in the foreseeable future.

It is evident from this discussion that the question of indivisibilities will be an acute one in airport investment. On the other hand quite small airports can be built initially and upgraded as time progresses. The question of indivisibilities has been especially marked in two cases. Firstly, newly independent nations which have wished to establish international airline links in the short term have been obliged to spend extremely large sums on airport facilities.[18] Secondly, the problem has appeared with the need to add to the existing capacity in major metropolitan areas.

Port Capacity

There are few seaports whose capacity to handle traffic is restricted by access to the landward or seaward side; for the great majority of seaports the capacity is determined by the number of berths and the available handling equipment. Even such data is insufficient as a measure of port capacity unless the type of traffic, the efficiency of port operation and the scheduling of shipping calls are also specified. The number of berths available in a port complex gives perhaps the best general measure of port capacity. Most general cargo berths can handle about 120 000 tons per annum, allowing for short periods of vacant berth, and assuming a mixed general cargo. The figure can be greatly increased if the cargo is containerised or palleted, perhaps to 250 000 tons per annum, depending upon the handling equipment available. A fully containerised system of ships, cargo and handling equipment can handle traffic of the order of 750 000 tons per annum.[19]

It is of course possible to install machinery for the handling of certain commodities in bulk. This results in a marked increase in capacity but a reduction in the flexibility of the port operation. The extreme case of this is a tanker terminal which can handle great tonnages of petroleum or similar products but cannot handle general cargo. Specialised berths within a port complex will similarly increase port capacity but reduce flexibility in port operation.

A critical limit to the type of vessels using a port may be imposed by the navigational conditions in access channels, especially the depth

of water. Such limits on the draught of ships using a port either pro-
hibit certain vessels from entering, or prevent them from entering
when fully laden with cargo. This type of limitation has always been
important in delta and estuarine ports, despite heavy expenditure
on dredging and pilotage services.[20] The problem has recurred with
the super-tankers. These vessels of over 400 000 tons are frequently
unable to enter even major ports, partly because of excessive draught,
partly because of poor manoeuvrability. Indeed it is clear that many
established oil ports in Europe will cease to be of primary importance
if present trends continue, and whole seas may well cease to be available for navigation by such vessels. There are of course various
solutions to the problem. One method is to use a large vessel with
transshipment to feeder tankers for distribution. Such transshipment
may take place in the open sea or at a special transshipment port
(Bantry Bay in southern Eire, for example, acts as transshipment
port for petroleum to other British Isles ports), or an established
port may adopt a transshipment function (a role which has for a
long time been important to Rotterdam's Europoort).

6.2 TECHNICAL PROPERTIES: SPEED AND TIME

The time taken to move a standard unit of some commodity between
two points on a network may be solely a function of distance, and thus
of network morphology, but in most cases other factors intervene
to cause marked variation in speeds.

Operating Speeds

Maximum operating speeds on a network are determined by considerations of safety, taking into account the network design and the
amount and character of traffic. These safety considerations may be
reinforced by operating regulations or legal sanctions. The maximum
operating speed for an individual vehicle on the network may be
further limited by its own technical specifications. For these reasons
it is seldom useful to specify one operating speed for the whole
network: it is necessary to identify the speed which can be maintained
in particular links of the network under normal operating conditions subject to reasonable safety limits and current legal restrictions.

In railway networks the maximum operating speed of high-
powered locomotives is in excess of 100 mph, but there are few routes

on which this is achieved. Firstly, there are often design limitations of the network, dating from an earlier period, which reduce speed over steep gradients or through sharp curves. Secondly, there is usually a slower traffic sharing the same track, and the precautions necessary to ensure reasonable safety margins lead to great reductions in operating speed.

In road networks the maximum speeds for most vehicles are lower, of the order of 70 mph, but the large number of independent operating units and the freedom they enjoy, at junctions for instance, cuts average operating speeds still further. In some cases the restriction is imposed by traffic conditions alone, but speed limits may also be enforced. In addition there are particular parts of the network whose narrowness, gradients or sharp bends further reduce operating speeds. It is the aim of motorway design to increase operating speeds by the elimination of steep gradients and sharp curves and by the reduction of hazards due to junctions and two-way traffic. The extent to which the resulting motorway actually increases average speeds is largely dependent on the density and heterogeneity of traffic.

In most water transport speeds are determined entirely by ship design, but in a few cases there are additional restrictions. In congested waters it may be necessary to reduce speeds in order to minimise collision risk. In rivers and canals speed limits may be imposed to protect the banks, while the mechanics of lock operation introduce another check on overall operating speeds. In air transport the limits are those of aircraft design and congestion in the vicinity of large airports.

Waiting Times

The second important element in the time taken to move consignments, and to a lesser extent passengers, is waiting time. Waiting time may occur either at terminals or *en route*. Waiting at terminals will occur wherever there are scheduled services, but also where a given consignment is only a small proportion of a complete vehicle load. Waiting *en route* may be due to congestion, but the most important category is delay caused by the need for sorting in marshalling yards and goods sheds. The extent of this delay is emphasised by the Beeching Report on British Railways, which reckoned an average origin–destination time of $1\frac{1}{2}$–2 days for an origin–destination distance of 67 miles.[21] The same report outlined one solution to this problem: liner trains of permanently coupled flat trucks (for containers) plying a regular schedule between a limited number of terminals.[22] Such a solution is only viable on routes with a high traffic density. At the same time the report suggested a great reduction in the number of stations handling freight, a suggestion which has been implemented over the past few years, with a target of 100 main freight depots.[23]

The terminal waiting times in sea transport are often very high, and when transshipment occurs *en route* another lengthy delay may be expected. This can be attributed to the fact that few consignments amount to a shipload, and scheduled services are infrequent except on a few high traffic routes. A further cause of delay in international shipping is the need for complex documentation procedures to be observed and for necessary clearances to be obtained. Terminal waiting time is very much lower in air and road transport, as operating units are smaller and scheduled services more frequent.

At first sight those differences might be thought unimportant except for the minority of commodities which are perishable and for certain categories of passenger traffic. In fact differences in speed have considerable significance for both freight and passenger traffic. Goods in transit represent working capital of the consignor or consignee. This capital is a scarce commodity and must therefore be costed either at the interest rate paid by the entrepreneur or as the opportunity cost of not investing that capital at market rates. In circumstances where capital is rationed or interest rates are very high these costs can be a high proportion of the total costs of transport; they will therefore affect both the level of transport demand and the choice of transport medium.[24] For example, groundnuts can be shipped from northern Nigeria to export ports by rail, river or road transport. The freight rates charged by the competing media are broadly competitive, but the road transport is able to achieve much speedier delivery and thus a greater turnover of limited capital.[25]

The implications for passenger movement are similar. The times spent by individuals in travelling can be valued in terms of average or opportunity costs. There is clear evidence that an implicit valuation of this type is frequently made by passengers in their choice of mode and route. For example the decision to use a toll bridge rather than a 'free' but circuitous route implies such a calculation. Similarly where a toll road runs parallel to a main road there are seldom any operating savings except in terms of time costs.

6.3 ECONOMIC PROPERTIES: COSTS

It is common knowledge that the costs of moving a standard unit of a commodity over a given distance are variable. They vary from one region to another, between routes within a region and even between directions on the same route. This variation can arise from geographical differences in the costs of network provision, from variation in the costs of vehicle operation, or from the policy adopted in recouping costs from the final consumer.

Geographical Variations in the Costs of Network Provision

The capital costs of network provision vary greatly for a number of reasons (figure 6.5). Firstly, the type of terrain through which the route is to be constructed will affect the cost of cuttings, embankments, bridges and so on.[26] Secondly, the inputs for construction may vary in cost, for example if the only source of aggregate is remote from the construction site. Thirdly, there may be variations in site acquisition costs; in some areas they are a very small proportion of total costs but in urban motorway construction the compensation for land and other adverse effects far exceeds the costs of construction itself.[27] These categories of costs are also influenced by the design standards adopted by the decision makers. If the design standards are for low volumes at low speeds, with high maintenance and operating costs, the capital costs can be minimised, but where design standards are better capital costs will rise.[28] The impact of these capital costs on the transport user will depend upon the interest charges and amortisation rate adopted. In a few cases these costs are partly or entirely met out of some extraneous account, but in most cases some part at least of construction costs will be borne by the transport user.

The current costs of network provision will be variable in a similar way. Part of this variation can be attributed to the variation in inputs (such as wage rates for maintenance staff), part to variations in the physical conditions, especially climate (such as the incidence of frost, snow and torrential rain), part to variations in wear and tear (and therefore proportional to traffic volume) and part again to the original design specifications. These recurrent costs, added to the charges on capital, represent the expenditure which the provider of the network must cover in the long term. In theory these costs may be met entirely from extraneous sources such as general taxation,

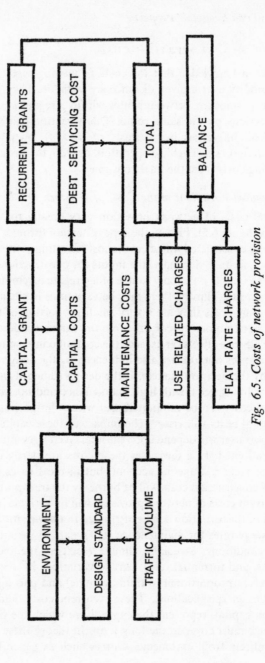

Fig. 6.5. Costs of network provision

but in practice a proportion at least is recouped from transport operators.

Recouping Network Costs

In designing devices to recoup this expenditure the most equitable procedure would be to levy charges proportional to the amount and location of network use (a high or low-cost area). Such discrimination is possible in some cases. For example most ports recoup a portion of their costs from charges which are levied for each entry to the port and scaled according to the net registered tonnage of the vessel.[29] A highly discriminating system can be maintained if the charges so raised are a small proportion of the operators' total costs but will tend to inhibit traffic where the proportion is higher.

The use of tolls is also a common method of charging for a specific facility in proportion to the use of it by an operator. Thus toll roads, toll bridges and canal tolls allowed the builders to recoup their costs from users, and the rates could be varied according to the construction and maintenance costs of a specific part of the network. The effective use of such tolls is dependent upon the ability to control entry and exit to the network, and the costs of collecting the tolls may become prohibitively expensive. For these reasons toll roads and bridges have become less familiar features of road transport in recent years, although technical innovations have suggested that electronically operated metering devices may become an effective method of road pricing in congested urban areas.[30]

The more common solution has been to abandon place-specific charges in favour of two alternatives. A licence fee for use of the network, at a flat rate per annum, can recoup costs but it makes no discrimination according to use unless it is a crude distinction based on weight or horsepower. Such charges are relatively cheap to collect. If the individual licensing areas are small some element of place-specific charges can be retained, but in general the license charges are identical for large areas of the network. The result is an element of cross-subsidy, by those who use low-cost areas of the network to those who use high-cost sections. The second alternative is to tax an essential operating input such as fuel. In this way the charge becomes proportional to use, but not weighted by location, except where the tax is calculated for very small geographic units, and then the possibilities of tax avoidance increase. In practice the level of such taxes is constant for large areas of the network. These two alternatives can of course be used in combination and then fulfil the conditions for a satisfactory two-part tariff argued by Lewis.[31]

Geographical Variation in Operating Costs

In these ways the variations in the costs of network provision are made part of the costs of transport operation. In addition, however, the operator will have costs, some of which may be geographically variable (figure 6.6).

Two categories of variation are identifiable: variation in the unit costs of operating inputs and variation in the technical efficiency of operation as measured by input–output ratios for quantities of input per ton mile performed. Variations in the unit costs of inputs will affect all supplies and labour. Thus fuel costs will vary internationally and even in some cases intranationally.[32] Similarly there will be international and interregional differences in the costs of labour for operation and maintenance.

The variations in the technical efficiency of operation, as measured by an input–output ratio, may arise in three ways. In the first place, they may arise from differences in network quality which themselves result from design decisions in a specific environmental context. Secondly, there may be environmental conditions, especially climatic conditions, which directly affect the efficiency of operation. Finally, there may be inefficiency imposed by traffic congestion on the network.

In railway transport little attention has been paid to variations in network quality except where some gross feature, such as an incline demanding the stationing of an auxiliary locomotive, is present.[33] This is probably due to the fact that network costs far exceed movement costs in most networks. For example, the figures provided in the Beeching Report on British Railways revealed that fuel, water and lubricants only constituted 9 per cent of total costs.[34] On the other hand the decisions explained in a later report took careful note of ruling gradients and speed restrictions in deciding between competing routes.[35] Similarly, little note is taken of climatic conditions which affect operating efficiency except where there is some exceptional feature to be remarked.[36] The effect of congestion on railway operation is most marked in terms of route capacity but may show in reduced operating speeds and therefore lower output.

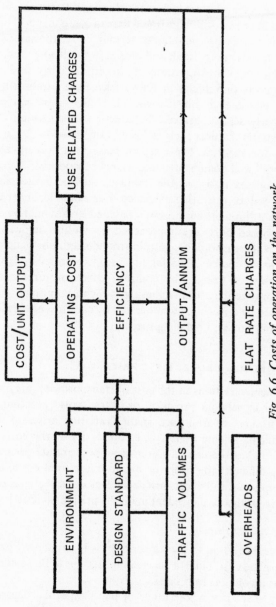

Fig. 6.6. Costs of operation on the network

The three categories are well marked in road transport. Studies in the United States have demonstrated that all components of operating cost are increased in mountainous terrain.[37] At the same time the operating speeds are reduced, and output (ton-miles per vehicle-hour or per man-hour) is proportionately lower. Similarly studies of the operating costs of vehicles in East Africa have demonstrated that operating efficiency is much lower on earth roads than on those with properly sealed surfaces.[38] Reduction in operating efficiency due to climatic features such as heavy rain, snow or fog is evident but little documented. The steep increase in delays on congested roads is both well documented and widely experienced.[39]

In air and sea transport the terminals may be limited in such a way as to reduce operating efficiency. For example, short runways may place a limit on an aircraft's payload and similar restrictions will occur when ports are approached by shallow channels. In the same media there is some congestion around major ports and airports, but the major source of variability in operating costs is climatic. Aircraft may be delayed by contrary winds or turbulence, both reducing productivity and increasing fuel consumption.[40] Deep-sea shipping can be affected by weather and by currents, again increasing fuel consumption and reducing speeds.

6.4 ECONOMIC PROPERTIES: PRICING

Geographical variations in the cost of transportation may therefore arise either in network provision or in transport operation, but for many customers of transport, spatial variation arises in the third sector, that of pricing policy. The complexity of the costs already discussed makes the identification of an appropriate pricing policy extremely difficult: the operator has to cover total costs, but both total receipts and total costs are dependent upon the level of traffic, which may in turn be dependent upon the pricing policy adopted.

Marginal Cost Pricing

The classical solution to such a problem is to argue that price must equal marginal cost, but in a penetrating analysis of this dictum Lewis notes that it contains four flaws.

Firstly, 'there is a whole range of marginal costs, depending on how far ahead one looks'.[41] This can be illustrated by an example in airline transport. Suppose an aircraft can take a maximum of 100 passengers. The marginal cost of the 100th passenger is almost zero but the marginal cost of the 101st would be a second aircraft. The significance of marginal costs is dependent upon the existence of excess capacity. Similarly with a railway system the marginal cost of each additional train on a track is low until capacity (in train paths per day) is reached; at that stage, an additional train will demand major network improvements at extremely high marginal cost.

Secondly, marginal cost will fluctuate from time to time. This is clearly a consequence of the previous point. Whenever demand falls below capacity marginal costs fall, but when demand rises above capacity marginal costs rise sharply. This is clear from a consideration of the commuter problem in which not only do marginal costs change rapidly (from 8 a.m. to 10 a.m., for example) but they differ at the same time on the same route in different directions. The third point is that indivisible escapable costs must be covered. A railway station is an indivisible escapable cost; it can be closed (therefore escapable), but if open it incurs a minimum cost (the indivisibility). The method of avoiding this is to redefine the rule: 'where there are indivisible expenses prices should not be less than the marginal cost. . . and the undertaking should not be continued unless the surplus over the divisible costs covers the indivisible expenses'.[42]

Lewis notes that definitions used in economics do not necessarily reflect those used in commercial accounting. (There are two riders to be added to this discussion: firstly, that the clerical costs of identifying these categories of cost may be excessive; secondly, that for adequate management and financial control, rates will often have to be decided and perhaps published in advance.)

If an operator is in a monopoly position, he can discriminate between traffic in the application of the principle outlined above, by varying the contribution which is made to covering indivisibilities. This power to discriminate may be limited by law, by the threat of competition or by what is deemed socially acceptable. The most effective monopolies of this type occurred in the early stages of railway development. There have however been many other monopolies, or collusive oligopolies, in other forms of transport at different periods. For example many shipping routes of the world are dominated by liner conferences; a group of shipping lines within a conference agrees on the number of sailings, the ports of call, the freight rates charged and a number of other details. [43] They endeavour to prevent competition by paying a loyalty rebate to those shippers who use none but the conference vessels. This loyalty rebate may be further strengthened by delaying its payment. Similarly, the International Air Transport Association acts as a rate fixing cartel in which competition is limited to specific aspects of standard of services. [44]

Types of Discrimination

Discrimination between commodities is often adopted in railway and shipping tariffs. Although this can sometimes be justified in

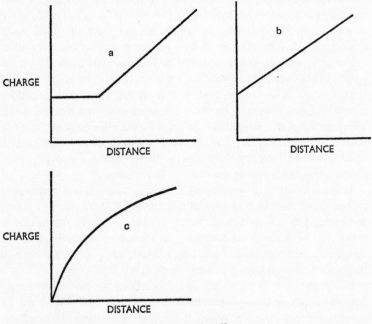

Fig. 6.7. Tariffs

terms of differences in handling costs—rubber latex, for example, is a difficult commodity to handle—it is more often based on consideration of 'what the traffic will bear', with a weather eye kept open for possible competition. It is argued that a high-value product can bear relatively high transport charges, while low-cost commodities cannot be expected to cover more than their marginal costs. Such discrimination may have marked implications for location theory. For example the shipping rates for processed commodities from West Africa to Europe are higher than those of the raw material; this tends to reinforce Europe's dominance of the processing industry.[45]

In some cases the principle has been extended to the direction of traffic. This may be based on arguments of excess capacity, but it may be simple discrimination. For example in 1968 the United States Maritime Commision ruled that there was an unjustifiable discrimination between east–west and west–east traffic on the North Atlantic in favour of the former.[46]

Another form of discrimination is based on the point of origin or destination. Once again the discrimination may be based on costs— for example, the shipping lines may load the tariffs to to ports in which navigational or cargo handling problems involve delays. On other occasions the concession may be a response to commercial or political pressure. Smith has demonstrated that the tariffs charged for stations in the Victoria–New South Wales border area of Australia were designed to 'pull' these towns within the commercial orbit of Melbourne, and counter-measures were instituted by Sydney.[47]

A common feature of tariffs is based on an important aspect of operator costs. Any consignment incurs certain costs of documentation and handling regardless of the distance it is moved. A series of devices can be used to recoup this cost, especially a minimum charge, a terminal charge and a taper; these can be used singly or in isolation. The effect of these devices (see figure 6.7) is to reduce average ton-mile costs with distance moved. In administering tariffs it is clear that continuously varying rates are difficult to use, so the normal method adopted is to have a series of distance bands within which a particular rate applies, often known as a stepped tariff.[48] In deep-sea shipping also it is common to quote a fixed tariff to a number of similarly located destinations even though their distances may differ slightly.

7 Vehicle Supply

The problems of network supply are often allowed to overshadow the equally important questions of vehicle supply: shipping, railway rolling stock, aircraft, motor vehicles. This can be attributed in part to the short working life of any unit of capacity and in part to the geographic mobility of vehicles. The implication of these two characteristics, in theory, is that supply should adjust rapidly to demand in both time and space and therefore no problems of significance should remain. The first section constitutes an attempt to explore in greater depth the spatial distribution of vehicle supply and the types of explanation which may be advanced. The succeeding section concerns the special case of public service capacity and its allocation to specific nodes and routes.

7.1 THE SPATIAL DISTRIBUTION OF VEHICLE CAPACITY

The description of the distribution of vehicle supply presents intractable problems. This is partly due to inadequacies of data sets, but it is also due to certain conceptual uncertainties in defining the quantities of interest.

The first major problem lies in defining the best measure of capacity. It is only in the case of motor vehicles that a single unit of capacity is an acceptable measure. In all other cases it is meaningless to use vehicle units, as the capacity of individual units is highly variable. Thus in shipping it is usual to refer not to the number of vessels but to the net registered tonnage of vessels registered in a country or plying a certain trade.[1] Similar problems are present with measurement of aircraft capacity, and for passenger aircraft the passenger capacity is probably the best unit of measurement. Similar problems are present with railway rolling stock and road freight vehicles. Consideration of these data leads to a further problem that the measure of capacity may well be less useful than a measure of output, for example potential ton-mileage per annum. In the case of shipping tonnages already referred to this would weight statistics and discriminate between obsolescent vehicles, with low operating speeds and high terminal times, and modern vessels with lower terminal times and higher operating speeds. On the other hand it must be acknowledged that such measures of output potential would fail to recognise that the efficiency with which the capacity can be used will be dependent upon network conditions and other external factors.

Similar problems arise from the question of location. Conceptually it is possible to identify three types of location definition: location of ownership, location of use and location of registration. It is the last of these which is most commonly available, for example with motor vehicles, aircraft and shipping. It is also the least valuable information, because the location of registration may bear no relation to the place of use or of effective ownership. This is a common aspect in international shipping where vessels are registered under 'flags of convenience', usually in order to take advantage of less stringent taxation, safety or labour regulations.[2] For this reason many United Kingdom registered vessels are operated in western Pacific waters, while oil tankers controlled by Greek interests and registered in Panama may never in the ordinary course of trade touch the shores of either country. It seems that the most important useful statistic is area of use but such data are hard to obtain. Similar problems occur in the mapping of aircraft capacity.

In studies of rail transport there is a stronger likelihood of ownership, registration and use being geographically coincident, although there may be short-term transfers of capacity to other areas. Indeed in the United States some smaller companies, in terms of track mileage and traffic, received substantial revenue from the hire of rolling stock to other companies on a *per diem* or mileage basis.[3]

Studies of road vehicle capacity face similar problems, although international registrations will usually be accurate enough. On a sub-national scale of study there will be a false emphasis on some centres of nominal ownership, double counting (where vehicles must be registered in every area of operation) and many significant effects due to the location of registration district boundaries. Once again the data must be treated with great caution.

Types of Explanation

In essence there are four main elements in the explanation of spatial patterns of vehicle capacity. The most basic element is the demand for transport. The second element is the availability of funds for the supply of capacity. The third element is the presence of complementary facilities, and finally there is the competitive element of alternative facilities. The problem is twofold: to identify a suitable measure for these variables, and to identify a suitable framework of explanation for their interaction upon one another.

Discussion in earlier chapters has already demonstrated the complexity of transport demand and the difficulties inherent in its measurement. For this reason specific demand functions have not been used as an independent variable in studies of spatial capacity supply. Similarly there is no simple way of estimating the funds available for the purchase of capacity. As a result a number of studies have tended to use a more general measure of economic activity as a surrogate for both these aspects—for example GNP *per capita*. The identification of suitable measures of complementary facilities —for example network mileage—presents few problems. There is however an important logical problem. It might be assumed that vehicle capacity and network capacity will be positively associated, but there is the special case in which improvement of the network facilities would allow the same demand to be met with smaller vehicle capacity. The presence of competitive facilities raises few problems of measurement in concept although exact definition may be difficult in certain cases.

The most widely used device for relating these determinants to vehicle capacity in geographic space is correlation and regression analysis. This theoretically agnostic tool also raises severe technical problems, including the need to standardise geographical units of investigation[4] and the problem of spatial autocorrelation.[5] Even if these technical problems can be overcome there are problems in interpreting the regression coefficients.

A different contribution to the problem was made by Lewis in his study of ocean freight rates. He argued that the difference between freight rates in one area and those in another should never exceed the costs of moving capacity from the one area to another in ballast. He argued that this price-equilibrating transfer would be facilitated by the presence of tramp shipping—vessels with no fixed route or commodity trade. Although this category of shipping has declined, the improvements in communications and the creation of a world market for shipping should have the same effect today. Lewis did not consider the level of vehicle supply, nor the movements of capacity, but the levels of freight rates in the various 'trades'. His empirical results were not altogether consistent with *a priori* reasoning.[6] (Lewis's paper is of importance also in that it was one of the earliest attempts to establish the existence of spatial price equilibrium. It has been neglected by location theorists presumably because it dealt with sea-space and not land-space, and with a form of capacity rather than a commodity.)

The Geographical Distribution of Motor Vehicle Capacity

The distribution of motor vehicle capacity is the most widely studied example for two reasons: the crude data, with limitations, are readily available; and it has wide relevance to planning problems.

An examination of the world distribution of motor vehicles, as for example in Ginsburg's atlas,[7] illustrates the wide variations in vehicle supply. It is evident that much of this variation can be explained in terms of population (representing demand) and wealth (representing supply factors). First, a large population mass has high transport demands for the movement of persons, food and industrial goods. A high level of wealth is necessary if these demands are to be met to any degree by road transport. There is moreover a general association between economic development and vehicle ownership identified historically by Rostow[8] and spatially by Owen.[9]

A statistical analysis of these associations at a continental scale has been attempted by Silberston. He chose automobiles per head as the dependent variable and income per head (supply or demand?), population density (presumably as a demand surrogate) and railway density (competing facilities?) as independent variables. The strongest single variable was income per head, but multiple regression showed positive coefficients for all three variables. This is in accordance with *a priori* reasoning on income and population density but contrary to it for railway route density (*a priori* reasoning specified railways as competitive transport forms, and a negative regression coefficient was therefore expected). The distribution of negative residuals highlighted the political restrictions on vehicle ownership in eastern Europe.[10]

On the intranational scale similar patterns of association are observed, but once again anomalies occur. Moreover, the mobility of motor vehicles leads to greater inconsistencies in the data as between place of registration and place of use. This can be illustrated from the West African case where the capital cities of Lagos, Accra and Abidjan each have an excessive proportion of total registrations. In the United Kingdom the variations of vehicle capacity were discussed by Sleeman,[11] and have more recently been discussed by Tanner[12] and Wagle[13]. Both these latter scholars depend upon regression techniques to establish simple and multiple correlations. Tanner used average income, social class, urbanisation, population density and 'distance north' to explain about 80 per cent of the observed variation of vehicles per head of population. Further research is evidently needed, if only to examine the implications of Tanner's curious 'distance north' variable in terms of other indices of standard of living and provision of services. The problem has also been investigated at a regional level. Hagerstrand has demonstrated that the distribution of vehicle ownership, at least in the initial stages, will reflect patterns of diffusion, but once this process is complete the distribution can be considered in static terms.[14] There is for example an immediate contrast between urban and rural areas.

Such variations of vehicle ownership within a rural area has been studied by Ajo for the area around Tampere in south central Finland.[15] Data were available by communes, and once again regression analysis was adopted as a statistical tool. A simple logarithmic regression on population identified two features of the distribution. Firstly, there was a general tendency for high levels of ownership around Tampere itself declining with distance from the town. Secondly, there were areas of excessively low ownership in the communes of Saaksmaki and Kuru. In the second stage of analysis vehicle ownership was related to economic potential, thus summarising both demand and supply factors. This proved a closer fit, and Ajo was able to identify 'unexplained variation' from residual values. He explained these in terms of the social and economic geography of the individual communes, and the effects of competing transport media.

Many studies have been made of vehicle ownership in urban areas, especially in the great metropolitan cities with their traffic planning problems. The explanation of these patterns has usually focused upon the marked increase in vehicle ownership with distance from the city centre which has been observed in Australia[16] and the United States. Shuldiner and Oi, for example, noted linear correlation coefficients of 0·533 in Chicago and 0·689 in Detroit.[17] The observed pattern can be interpreted in *a priori* terms. Transport demand increases with distance from the city centre, public services are usually less frequent in time and space, and the peripheries are often favoured as residential areas for the higher income groups. In the Australian case Scott acknowledges the importance of these factors and suggests also the influence of traffic congestion and the costs of garage space for vehicle owners in the city centre.[18] The argument has been extended by Lansing and Hendricks in the United States. They

conclude that the character of the urban environment does have a substantial influence on automobile ownership, and that this influence takes two forms. It holds down the proportion who own any car among those in the lower part of the income distribution. . . and the proportions who own two or more motor cars among those in the upper part.[19]

It is evident that this pattern, and indeed the diffusion of multiple ownership, will determine vehicle ownership within the great cities of the developed countries in the next decade.

7.2 SCHEDULED SERVICES

In most freight transport systems the pattern of vehicle movement is closely tied to demand, and capacity is held idle, rescheduled or rerouted at will. For a few freight systems and for most passenger systems, however, there are scheduled services with routes and time-tables specified in advance. This spatiotemporal allocation of vehicle supply is sometimes assumed to be trivial for two reasons: it is thought that the allocation of capacity will simply match demand (empirical research and everday experience throw doubt on this belief); secondly it is assumed that the pattern is formed by a multitude of decisions in negotiation between interested parties and the the results can only be explained in idiographic terms. The contrary view sees the pattern as one of considerable importance worthy of careful analysis and capable of general explanation.

Patterns of Public Service Provision

The pattern of public services has been subject to a number of studies using cartographic techniques. Most of these studies have been based upon the concept of accessibility to a specified point or small number of points, and have thus failed to describe the pattern as

a whole. In order to combine the elements of service availability
in both space and time Forbes has suggested the use of 'access time'
which is the sum of mean journey time and mean terminal waiting
time.[20] In this way a point with frequent but indirect services would
be deemed more accessible than one with direct service at very
infrequent intervals. Although such studies are of value in specific
circumstances they have not proved fruitful in a wider context.

In many respects service networks are analogous to route networks,
and the same properties of density, access, distance, can be applied
both to the service network and to its access points. The graph
theoretic measures of network form also can be applied to the network
of scheduled services. A number of studies made by Haggett and his
associates have focused upon the study of airline route patterns.[21]
Their findings have confirmed the doubts already expressed by Werner
and have led them to suggest a classification of network form based
upon the frequency distribution of paths in a shortest path matrix.[22]
The published findings are suggestive but not conclusive evidence
that the method proposed is superior. Similarly the factor analysis
of the Venezuelan airline network by Garrison and Marble is a fruitful
approach to detecting secondary structure within a network. Their
much-quoted study distinguished four factors which they interpreted
as the number of destinations served from each node, the general
'field' of connections to Caracas, the presence of regional subsystems
and regional subsystems at two scales.[23]

Reed has attempted to extend the analysis still further in a study
of the Indian airline network.[24] Once again the first stage was the
construction of a binary connectivity matrix and the derivation of
a minimum path matrix for the whole system. From this he calculated
the mean graph distance of each vertex from all other vertices. The
contribution of each major network node to this pattern was then
assessed by 'removing' it and its links from the system and recalculating
the mean graph distances. Such a removal resulted in a general increase
in graph distances, and in some cases the removal of some nodes
from all contact resulting in an increase in the number of sub-graphs.
These effects were measured by the average change in the mean
graph distances, regardless of sign. In the Indian example the original
network of 39 nodes had an average graph distance of 2·30. The
mean change caused by the removal of Bombay was 0·412, of Calcutta
0·256, of Delhi 0·115, of Madras 0·115, and so on. Reed interpreted

this as a measure of 'dominance' in the system.[25] The techniques suggested by Reed, though lacking in theoretical elegance, appear to identify a further dimension of connectivity.

The use of simple binary connectivity matrices is flawed by the absence of any weighting by service frequency or carrying capacity. There are two approaches to this problem. The simplest is to construct binary matrices for different levels or frequencies of service. The general connectivity matrix already discussed could then be compared with that for daily services, or hourly services, using measures already discussed. In most cases the number of nodes and edges would be reduced. Such a technique is laborious and more fruitful of data than insight.

The alternative is to devise a system of weighting for the original connectivity matrix. For example, if the initial connectivity matrix is constructed to show the number of services available between two vertices in a given time period, then the nth power of the matrix will indicate the possibility of getting from vertex i to vertex j in n steps if the cell ij is positive, while the value in that cell will indicate the number of route and service combinations by which the journey could be achieved. This technique is useful but cannot of course ensure that all possible route and service combinations are also 'reasonable'.

Finally use may be made of a technique proposed by Nystuen and Dacey which is examined in more detail in a later chapter. The essence of the technique is to define the nodal flow from a given centre as the highest outgoing flow to a higher order centre. The nodal flows then mapped or analysed will evidently be much reduced in number and the overall pattern will be simplified. On the other hand the technique explicitly seeks hierarchical structures and will not necessarily identify other structures when no hierarchy is present.[26]

These various forms of empirical analysis have repeatedly identified two types of pattern. The first is the tendency for networks to form a number of subsystems. Contacts within the subsystems are easily made but contacts between the subsystems are poorly served both in the number of routes and the frequency of services. The subsystems often exhibit orientation towards a single node through which all external contacts are made. The presence of such subsystems in road passenger transport was explored by a number of studies in the 1950s, notably those by Green[27] and Godlund.[28] The identification of such patterns is often a by-product of urban hinterland and central-place studies.

The second, related, pattern is the tendency for the pattern of services to define a hierarchy of communications centres. Within this hierarchy an nth order centre will be directly linked to a small number of same order centres and to one higher order centre through which external links are established. A hierarchy of this type was identified by Snyder in Uruguay,[29] and is implicit in the results of airline analysis performed by Reed[30] and by Garrison and Marble.[31] A number of studies have suggested, explicitly or implicitly, that this communication hierarchy is isomorphic with the central-place hierarchy. This view is consistent with the emphasis of Christaller's original thesis[32] and is further strengthened by the observed association between population of settlements and the level of their external services.[33] For example, two studies in rural Yorkshire have emphasised this relation.[34] On the other hand the argument is two-edged. The transport system and the settlement system may indeed be interdependent, but in many cases the causation is circular: the form of the urban hierarchy may be influenced by the pattern of services, and the converse is equally true.

Determinants of Capacity Allocation

The explanation of capacity allocation must be initially formulated in terms of the operators' response to demand. But this response is subject to a number of technical, economic and industrial restrictions. Once again the choice of a measure for demand is extremely difficult. Although demand functions can be estimated for particular routes they are seldom used either in decision making or in explanatory studies. Similarly, although it is possible to specify the types of political and economic restrictions operating in a specific case, it is difficult to formulate any general statement. For this reason most attempts at explanation have used crude surrogate variables for demand, and residuals from the observed relation are explained in idiographic terms.[35]

The design of a service schedule is extremely complex. The object is to provide a specified level of service capacity between specified nodes at specified times. This object must be achieved with the minimisation of empty running and passenger interchange, and with the smallest possible vehicle stock. The minima may be mutually incompatible. Finally the system will have certain constraints of which the most important is the cyclic element: the whole pattern is repeated on a weekly, daily or some similar basis, and at the end of each cycle the system must return to an initial state. Early methods of timetabling have been largely replaced by methods of operations research to solve the complex problems involved.[36]

The result of such computations will inevitably include the 'balancing' movement of capacity on certain routes far in excess of the demand expressed at average prices. The simplest example of this is backhaul capacity, which frequently occurs, for example, in commuter systems. A second element of excess capacity may be due to indivisibilities. Suppose the capacity available consists of units each capable of handling thirty-five passengers, whether railway coaches, aeroplanes or buses. The capacity offered on a particular route will then be 'lumpy' (0 seats, 35 seats, 70 seats, and so on). These two elements will lead to excess capacity on certain routes at specified times; the third element will provide excess capacity at certain times in certain areas of the network but not on any particular route, because of temporal fluctuations in aggregate demand in the system.

When spare capacity of any of these three types is present, the decision as to its use will depend upon the balance of marginal costs and marginal revenue.

In the first two cases, as the vehicles are already committed to movement, the additional costs of opening them to traffic will be very small indeed, and any traffic which can be attracted at a rate above this marginal cost will be profitable. For this reason the operator may seek to devise special charges to attract such additional traffic, although he will also seek to frame the concession in such a way that 'normal' traffic is unable to take advantage of it. If, on the other hand, the capacity is in the third category, the marginal costs of using it will be much greater—it will include all those costs which are related to distance moved, such as fuel, lubricants or wear and tear—and the charges made will have to be proportionally greater. This type of operation accounts for many services in low demand areas at off-peak periods.

Another economic justification for operating excess capacity on low demand routes is the feeder concept. Suppose the branch route in question contributes traffic to the main system which, if charged at normal rates, would either fall to zero or be lost to some competing system: in that case the marginal analysis can be extended to include the total marginal revenue and expenditure for the traffic, on both branch route and main system. Such an analysis may reveal that it is profitable to operate feeder services with very low load factors, even with concession charges.

Most passenger services are subject to regulation by local, national or international authorities. The most common form of intervention has the effect of restricting companies. The most extreme case is the grant of an exclusive monopoly over certain routes or in certain regions. This is the most common form of road passenger regulation in the United Kingdom;[37] it is also widely used by nations to protect their internal airlines. In exchange for the monopoly the operator may agree to certain standards of service, fare levels, routes served, and so on. Less extreme is the granting of operating licences to a small number of operators who are expected to compete on certain aspects while other aspects are fixed by the licensing authority. The Civil Aeronautics Board in the United States,[38] the Air Transport Licensing Board in the United Kingdom and much of the International Air Transport Association regulation is of this type.[39] At the other extreme can be found completely unregulated systems, as for example in Nigeria's passenger road services.

The rationale for such regulations is seldom clearly presented. In some cases it is argued that regulation is necessary to maintain standards of services, such as safety; it is not clear that this aim is achieved, and the same aim could be achieved by stringent regulation without monopoly powers. In other cases it is argued that only the grant of monopoly will attract sufficient capital into a risky enterprise. In yet other cases the regulation is used to maintain less profitable parts of the network as a *quid pro quo* for the granting of profitable operating rights elsewhere. Implicit in such arrangements is the concealed cross-subsidy of one service by another, or at least a discriminating allocation of overhead costs. This type of reasoning appears to have been prominent in the operation of the US Civil Aeronautics Board and in much bus service licensing in the United Kingdom.

8 Patterns of Transport Flow

It has already been noted that flow data may be used to classify network facilities on a functional basis. There is in addition a case for studying the pattern of flow itself. Traditionally such analysis has adopted a cartographic method with the main patterns being identified and portrayed in map form,[1] but this method has proved unsatisfactory where flows are very complex, or where very large amounts of data have to be analysed. This has led to the adoption of new techniques for analysis, and to the disaggregation of flow data in order to explain smaller component parts of the whole.

8.1 BASIC PATTERN TYPES

Empirical research and cartographic analysis have for a long time recognised three basic geographical patterns of flow: blocks, hinterlands and hierarchies. The three categories are not mutually exclusive. An interaction block is defined as a group of geographical units with high internal interaction and low external interaction. The concept of an interaction block in this sense is well understood in studies of international trade, and the existence of such blocks is also clear in some flow maps. It is important to note also that interaction blocks may be made up of contiguous or non-contiguous geographical units. For example, the trading *blocs* of the first half of the twentieth century were based not on geographical proximity but on the political organisation of colonial empires.[2] On the other hand, the period since the second world war has seen the emergence of a number of political organisations whose role is to stimulate the development of an interaction block in a number of contiguous territories. Significant among these are Comecon, the European Common Market, and further afield, the Latin American Free Trade Area.[3] Although the concept of an interaction block is clear, the operational definition of its existence and its membership is more difficult.

117

The second spatial pattern is the *hinterland*: an area in which the dominant flows are convergent upon, or divergent from, a single geographic location. This concept is commonly used in studies of ports and or urban centres.[4] Once again the obvious cases are clear in cartographic analysis, but more complex patterns are common. In treating the complex patterns a distinction is often made between the exclusive hinterland or *umland* and the competitive hinterland which is shared with other ports or towns.[5] Studies of ports in highly developed areas suggest that exclusive hinterlands are very small and in many cases nonexistent. For example, statistics collected in the United Kingdom in 1964 revealed that even in the immediate vicinity of major ports a proportion of the traffic was diverted to other ports: only the import trades of Hull and Bristol exhibit any evidence of an exclusive hinterland.[6]

The third type of pattern is *hierarchical*. In many flow systems, products are collected through a hierarchy of assembling centres, and may be distributed in similar fashion. In a few cases, the entire hierarchy may represent an interaction block with very few flows to or from external locations. The political economy of Dahomey described by Polanyi was of this type.[7] A more common pattern is for these hierarchical systems to represent the first and last stages in the international or interregional trading system.[8]

In addition to these three pattern types there is the phenomenon known as distance decay.[9] In most flow systems, the greater the distance the less the volume of flow. The exact form of this relation appears to be extremely variable. The ubiquity of its presence and the variability of its form make it a phenomenon of little explanatory value, but it constitutes an empirical regularity with which any theoretical explanation of transport flow must be consistent.

8.2 METHODS OF ANALYSIS

A number of methods of analysis have been evolved to identify the presence of such patterns in complex flow systems. Most of these methods are 'neutral' in that they do not presuppose the presence of any particular type of pattern, but some methods are designed to identify a specific pattern type. Finally mention should be made of those studies which analyse a flow pattern in relation to some *a priori* theory of flow.

Transaction Flow Analysis

This technique was originally devised by Savage and Deutsch.[10] Suppose a flow system for which the total outgoing and incoming flows are known for all regions or centres. The expected flow under an assumption of origin–destination independence can then be predicted for any origin–destination pair as

$$Fe_{ij} = F_{i*} . F_{*j} . F_{**}^{-1} \qquad (8.1)$$

where Fe_{ij} is the expected flow from i to j
F_{i*} is the total outgoing flow from i to all regions
F_{*j} is the total incoming flow to j from all regions
F_{**} is the total flow in the system.

The relation of the expected flow to the actual flow (F_{ij}) can then be considered in a number of forms

$$\text{Difference} = F_{ij} - Fe_{ij} \qquad (8.2)$$

$$\text{Ratio} = F_{ij} (Fe_{ij}^{-1}) \qquad (8.3)$$

$$\text{Salience score} = RA_{ij} = (F_{ij} - Fe_{ij})(Fe_{ij}^{-1}) \qquad (8.4)$$

Maps of dyads with high differences, ratios or salience scores will then be used to identify the dominant pattern in the system.[11] The method is particularly suitable for the identification of interaction blocks. For example, value estimates of Nigeria's interregional trade in 1964 yielded the pattern of positive salience scores mapped in figure 8.1, emphasising the interdependence of the federation.[12]

Factor Analysis

Factor analysis and a number of related techniques were developed as a multivariate statistical classificatory method in a number of disciplines far removed from transport studies.[13] In essence the technique reduces a large number of observed variables to a much smaller number of 'factors'. It is possible to interpret a factor by observing on which variables it 'loads' heavily, and to classify the taxonomic units by their 'scores' on each factor. In aggregate flow studies the technique can be applied in two modes. The first stage is to draw up an origin–destination matrix with the volume of flows between them. This matrix can then be analysed in two ways: the R-mode is used to classify groups of destinations with similar supply patterns; conversely Q-mode classifies groups of origins with similar destination patterns or customers.[14] The method has been applied with great success in studies of India but its full range of capability has not yet been rigorously identified.[15]

Nystuen and Dacey's Nodal Flows

A number of scholars have attempted to define procedures for the identification of hierarchical structure in complex flow systems.

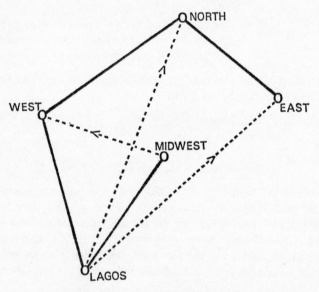

Solid line implies score positive in both directions; broken line implies score positive in direction indicated

Fig. 8.1. Salience scores for interregional trade in Nigeria
(after Smith)

Nystuen and Dacey's proposed method was originally applied to telehone traffic but has since been applied to commodity flows.[16]

Consider an origin–destination matrix of flows. The first stage consists of ranking the locations according to the total incoming flow. The second stage defines the *dominant* flow from each location as the largest outgoing flow. If this dominant flow is to a lower order centre the origin centre is termed *independent*, but if the dominant flow is to a higher order centre the flow is termed *nodal*. The nodal flows may then be mapped, and a range of patterns will result, from simple dominance of all centres by one centre, through an integrated hierarchy in which one centre dominates all other centres directly or indirectly, to an absence of hierarchy in which a large number of independent centres exists. (The resulting simplified matrix can also be treated as the binary connectivity matrix of a planar graph and the same techniques applied as have been discussed above.) Application of this technique to flows of rail traffic between 27 major Nigerian towns failed to yield a clear hierarchical pattern, suggesting that the tool is not only able to identify hierarchies but also to demonstrate their absence from some systems.[17]

8.3 DISAGGREGATED FLOW DATA

Where disaggregation by commodity is possible—usually a question of data sources—many of the techniques already discussed can be used to greater effect and a number of alternative approaches become possible.

Complementarity and Interdependence

This concept, which was first outlined by Ullman, has two facets.[18] At one level it is an explanation of flow systems; at a second it is a descriptive analytic device. Ullman argued from the familiar assertion that transport flows occur because of areal differentiation, to the more precise statement that flows occur when regions are specifically complementary—that is, for a given commodity one region is in surplus and the other is in deficit. Assuming that no commodities are destroyed Ullman has identified the same quantities as salience analysis, namely the outgoing and incoming flows of the respective regions. Although Ullman offers no formal algebra it can only be assumed that the complementarity between the two regions is proportional to the product of the two quantities (F_{i*} and F_{*j}). It is not possible from his verbal statement to decide whether the third quantity (F_{**}) would also become part of the formalisation. (A similar approach would be to define the greatest potential complementarity between regions i and j as being the smaller of the two quantities F_{i*} and F_{*j}.) The potential complementarity between regions, however calculated, can then be compared with the actual flow, as ratios, differences and so on, and the pattern of these values may be expected to identify an important pattern in the system.

Factor Analysis of Disaggregated Flow Data

Where a commodity breakdown is available it is possible to use factor analysis to classify origin–destination pairs (dyads) according to the commodity mix which they handle. Consider a flow with 10 regions and 10 commodities. This can be represented as a matrix of 90 (dyads) × 10 (commodities) or, if intraregional flows are included, of 100 × 10. Factor analysis of the matrix will allow the identification of commodity mixes (factors interpreted by loadings) and dyad groups (according to factor scores). Berry used this method to great effect in a 1260 × 63 matrix of flows in India. His interpretation of his results is illuminating.

The first factor records, for example, the northward and eastward flows of the specialities of Bombay and Madras ... Factor three looks at the flows of commodities originating in the east ... and also shows the *redistribution function of Madras*. Much of the complexity of factor four can be resolved into *port–hinterland* relationships between manganese producing areas and exporting ports. Factor five identifies movements *within the Bombay–Delhi region*. . . .[19]

The present author's italics emphasise that the technique was able to identify hierarchical, hinterland and block patterns within the broader system of flows.

Further Disaggregation of Commodity Flows

Smith and Hay have suggested that it is fruitful to disaggregate further and to break an internodal commodity flow into internodal links and strands (table 8.1), and a measurement of strand magnitude is readily available where there is access to a sample of waybills.[20] The data thus collected can be used to relate the study of transport to the study of trading systems. For example, it is commonly asserted that a town has the hierarchical function of bulking or breaking bulk, and this belief may be reinforced by a flow pattern which shows the same town with both inward and outward flows of the same commodity. The presence of bulking or break of bulk should be detectable in the strand magnitude pattern of the flows. If the pattern of inward flows does not differ significantly from that of outward flows, the role of the town must be redefined as one of staging but not of bulk-changing. Smith and Hay demonstrated the use of this technique for Nigerian railway traffic, and a comprehensive investigation has been prepared by Onakomaiya.[21]

TABLE 8.1

COMPONENTS OF COMMODITY FLOW SYSTEMS

Flow or connection	Terminals
Interregional flow	Producing and consuming areas
Internodal flow	Urban centres and transport terminals
Internodal links	Shippers at terminal nodes
Internodal strands	Consignments and receipts

Disaggregation of Passenger Flows

In passenger flow studies it is possible to identify a number of component flows or submarkets for passenger movement. Each of these component flows can then be analysed by salience scores, R and Q-mode factor analysis, nodal analysis, and so on. Furthermore, complementary nodes can be identified and dyads can be classified according to their pattern of traffic. The data may also be used to test assertions about the nature of a flow based on observation of its spatial pattern alone.

In such studies the most important problem is the identification of a suitable basis for classifying the submarkets. That most commonly used in urban studies has been trip purpose (work, school, shopping), but many other studies have also found it necessary to distinguish the occupation or socioeconomic status of the travellers.[22]

8.4 QUASI-EXPLANATORY ANALYSIS

There remains a group of studies which lie midway between analysis and explanation. Simple explanatory formulae are used to predict flows, and the important flows are deemed to be those which differ significantly from the prediction.

Distance-Based Analyses

Attention has already been drawn to the distance decay pattern and the possibility of fitting a variety of curves to this pattern. A more sophisticated approach utilises the two quantities F_{i*} and F_{*j} and the distance d_{ij} to predict the expected flows between two regions (Fe_{ij}), using equations of the forms

$$Fe_{ij} = k(F_{i*} . F_{*j})(d_{ij}^{-1}) \tag{8.5}$$

$$\text{or} \quad Fe_{ij} = (F_{i*} . F_{*j})(d_{ij}^{-a}) \tag{8.6}$$

$$\text{or} \quad Fe_{ij} = k(F_{i*} . F_{*j})(d_{ij}^{-a}) \tag{8.7}$$

Of these three equations the first is directly soluble, and the second is directly soluble in logarithms. The third is linear in logarithmic form; regression analysis can therefore be used to obtain the best fit line. So, for a large number of dyads, k or a or both can be estimated where appropriate. High positive and negative residuals may then be used to identify the presence of blocks, hierarchies, and so on. This approach, sometimes termed the interactance model, is closely related to the gravity model which will be examined in the following chapter.[23]

Analyses based on Population and Distance

A number of studies have sought to relate the volume of flows to population and distance alone. In passenger movement studies Cummings argued that flows could be predicted on the basis of two assumptions: all persons a given distance apart are equally likely to interact in a given time period; and given equal population densities a person is just as likely to take a trip d miles as d' miles. Under these assumptions the flow between 'the two nodes having n_i and n_j persons, separated by a distance d_{ij} ... [will] be proportional to $n_i . n_j . d_{ij}^{-1}$'. The ratio of actual flow to this predicted flow is termed by Cummings a normalised flow. He used the method to study airline passenger traffic in the United States.[24]

In commodity flow studies population has been used as a surrogate variable for demand in a number of studies. Smith reviews these applications and concludes that 'the surprising thing about the analyses of the volume of shipments described . . . is that the two variables in isolation, population and distance, perform as well as they do'.[25] Smith himself has used the two variables in an attempt to define Ullman's concept of complementarity. He defines the expected flow from i to j as the potential complementarity of the two regions

$$Fe_{ij} = (F_{i\bullet} P_j)(d_{ij}^{-1}) \tag{8.8}$$

where P_j is the population of the jth region. The relation between this expected flow and observed flow was then examined both as a simple ratio and as absolute residuals from a best fit regression line. The results of the second stage were mapped for Interstate Commerce Commission data for agricultural commodity shipments into New England.[26] Two comments can be made about this paper: the first is that because no road transport data were available, the data set was probably insufficient truly to test the idea which Smith puts forward. The second is that Smith's definition of complementarity is too different from Ullman's concept for the paper to be considered a test of Ullman's ideas.

9 The Explanation of Flow Systems

The task of this chapter is to identify the main types of explanation which have been offered for the form of flow systems. In one sense this question has already been tackled by the earlier chapters on the demand for transportation: flows occur where the demand for transportation is sufficient to ensure the supply of both network and vehicle capacity. The question must therefore be rephrased more broadly: what are the underlying determinants of flow patterns which are expressed both in the geographical pattern of transport demand and in the patterns of the flow themselves? This question can be approached from four different directions. The first approach is based upon geographical distributions and hence is concerned with proximate causes, the second approach is based in economic theory and results in the conclusion that the problem of flow is the inverse of the more familiar problems of location theory, the third approach has no theoretical presuppositions, while the fourth is eclectic in format.

9.1 THEORIES DEPENDENT UPON GEOGRAPHICAL DISTRIBUTIONS

The key assumption for this group of studies is that the geographical distribution of production and consumption or surplus and deficits can be used as *independent* variables in the study of flow generation. The validity of this assumption has already been implicitly challenged in an earlier section, but even if its general validity is not accepted the assumption may nevertheless be thought reasonable in a study of proximate causes.

Stamp insisted that land use studies provide a basis of explanation and policy.[1] The correlation between urban land use and traffic generation has been widely used as a basis of explanation and prediction in urban transport policy. Similar relationships can be observed between the social and economic characteristics of larger geographical areas and the traffic which they generate by road, rail or other media.[2]

An example of this type of work is provided by Starkie's study of the Medway towns.[3] He attempted to correlate traffic and land use for all industrial firms employing more than ten persons in the study area. Of the 91 relevant firms 77 provided data and gave permission for site traffic counts. Regression analysis revealed only a weak relationship between the traffic generated and the employment and floor space of the plants. The relationships revealed were curvilinear, a feature interpreted by Starkie as suggesting that 'Once the basic needs of a department have been met . . . traffic grows more slowly because any subsequent demand for movement . . . has its effects mainly by changing load factors of vehicles already scheduled to call at the plant'.[4] The analysis was then repeated for plants grouped according to the Standard Industrial Classification. Higher correlation coefficients were obtained and the orders of the classification were 'then ranked according to their position with reference to a standard trend line'.[5]

Although this method has been widely used in urban transport planning it is extremely unsatisfactory as an explanatory approach. In the first place it explains traffic generation and traffic attraction of areas, but not, in most cases, traffic generation between areas. Secondly, it is seldom that aggregate land use data can be related directly to traffic with a high degree of confidence. In most cases it is necessary to disaggregate the traffic and the land uses. Eliot-Hurst for example, in a study of traffic generation in Perth, found it necessary to carry out separate analyses for industrial floor space and commercial floor space as traffic generators within the central urban area.[6] Thirdly, it cannot be claimed that the observed associations are constant over space or time. In spatial terms the relationships observed in one city may differ strongly from those recorded in another. Similarly, in the long run increased transport costs, for example as a result of traffic congestion, may force a change either of technology or of location in order to reduce the traffic generated.

The Gravity Model

The so-called gravity model relies upon analogy with the Newtonian definition of gravity: that the attraction between two objects is proportional to the product of their masses and inversely proportional to the square of the distance between them. The revolutionary quality of the gravity model has been discussed by Hesse and this, combined with its great success in the physical sciences, made it an attractive analogy for social scientists.[7] Geographical studies have focused upon four problems in the application of the analogy: the inteepretation of the analogy, the specification of equivalents of mass and distance, and the choice of an exponent for the distance variable.[8]

The first users of the analogy sought no further justification for its adoption than that it proved a good fit to certain classes of data, especially migration data. More recently scholars have reacted to the suspicion that it has a weak theoretical basis and have sought a rigorous justification of its form.[9] Carroll and Bevis, for example, have demonstrated that the gravity equation for the interaction between two populations can be derived from simple probability linked to a distance decay function.[10] Firstly, the flow between two regions (*i* and *j*) can be predicted on the basis of origin–destination independence as

$$T_{ij} = (P_i P^{-1})(P_j P^{-1}) T_{**} = P_i P_j P^{-2} T_{**} \qquad (9.1)$$

where T_{ij} is the flow from *i* to *j*
T_{**} is the total flow in the system
P is the total population of the system
P_i is the population of the *i*th region
P_j is the population of the *j*th region.

Verbally, the flow between two subregions in a system is a proportion of total flow in the system determined by the product of the ratios of the population of each subregion to total population in the system. The second stage is empirically based. If a number of interaction studies relate T_{ij} (as defined above) to I_{ij} (the observed interaction or flow between the subregions) it is found that

$$I_{ij} = c \cdot T_{ij} \cdot d_{ij}^{-b} \qquad (9.2)$$

where c is a constant
d_{ij} is the distance between the subregions
b is an empirically derived exponent.

Simplifying and substituting these equations gives

$$I_{ij} = c \cdot P_i P_j \cdot P^{-2} \cdot T_{**} \cdot d_{ij}^{-b} \qquad (9.3)$$

but the quantities c, P and T_{**} are all known constants, so defining a new constant

$$G = c \cdot P^{-2} \cdot T_{**} \qquad (9.4)$$

then

$$I_{ij} = G \cdot P_i P_j \cdot d_{ij}^{-b} \qquad (9.5)$$

which is the general form of the gravity equation.

This derivation is attractive, but it must be noted that the specification of equations 9.1 to 9.5 involves a known T_{**}. If T_{**} is not known the equations can only specify the expected share that T_{ij} will have a total flow in the system, but not the expected flow in real terms.

A similar but stronger interpretation was offered by Wilson.[11] He started with 'the key assumption that all possible states of the system are equally probable . . . then the most probable estimate of I_{ij} is that which is produced by the greatest number of system states'.[12] Such an assumption is very similar to the origin–destination independence of Carroll and Bevis, and in isolation would yield trivial results. The critical stage of the analysis is the specification of a number of constraints specifying production, consumption, surpluses and deficits, or total flows in the system. It is these constraints which give form to the equation similar to that of the gravity model

$$I_{ij} = A_i \cdot B_j \cdot X_i \cdot Y_j \cdot f(c_{ij}) \qquad (9.6)$$

where for a given commodity

> X_i is production in region i
> X_j is consumption in region j
> A_i, B_j are derived
> $f(c_{ij})$ is some decreasing function of c_{ij}, the transport costs of one unit of commodity moving from i to j.

Although complex in derivation, Wilson's justification of the gravity equation is undoubtedly the strongest case for its retention yet made.

Finally it can be noted that some economists have recently sought an economic justification of the gravity model. Niedercorn and Bechdolt, for example, have attempted a derivation based upon utility theory.[13] If the net utility of a trip—the utility of the good or service acquired minus the disutility of trip making—is defined as a function of the number of trips from any origin i to destination j, it is possible to derive the gravity equations in utility maximising terms.

It is clear that the preferred derivation of the gravity equations will influence the choice of analogues for mass. Initial applications of the model in the social sciences were concerned with migrant and passenger flows, and the obvious analogue was the population total of the the origin and destination regions.[14] This has remained a feature of gravity model applications in such diverse fields as telephone traffic,[15] air traffic[16] and migrant flows. There is also a literature which seeks to define appropriate weights for the populations according to income. Other variables have been used in other applications.[17] Some commuter studies, for example, have used employed residents in the region of origin and employment in the region of destination.[18] The derivation suggested by Wilson justifies the use of total production (in region of origin) and consumption (in region of destination) for interregional commodity flow studies.[19]

Some authors have sought to contrast this method with interactance models. These are based on the assumption that only surpluses and deficits enter flow systems, and that surpluses and deficits are therefore the appropriate analogues for mass in the gravity equation. A commuter study would use the net surplus of residents over jobs in the origin zone and *vice versa* in the destination zone. The evident point to be made is that by this assumption the absence of surpluses and deficits would indicate the elimination of flow. Evidence suggests that this conclusion is false: cross flows do occur even if surpluses and deficits are absent. Furthermore, A. G. Wilson has demonstrated that the distinction is largely illusory and that the interactance case can be viewed as a specially constrained case of the gravity model.[20]

The distance parameter raises similar questions of definition and measurement. At first sight the costs of overcoming distance appear to be satisfactory, but they are complex. Any costs of movement must recognise not only the fares or freight rates but also the time cost of the exercise. In the case of passenger movement, time may be valued at the average rate or the marginal rate, either for the population as a whole or for the sector of the population actually involved in travelling.[21] Alternatively the time spent in travelling can be assessed empirically by calculating the amount of money which specific travelling groups are prepared to pay for an increase in journey speed. In freight studies the costs of time are too often ignored, but real costs are incurred in inventories both of goods in transit and of stocks at terminals.[22] Once again this cost, a capital cost, may be charged at the average, the marginal or the opportunity costs of interest. Furthermore, where vehicle ownership is involved, it is necessary to distinguish between the marginal and average costs of making a particular movement. Finally it can be noted that distance may also involve a behaviour or information aspect.[23] Suppose that the amount of information declines with distance in a consistent manner; then interaction with distant trading partners, or movement to more distant jobs, will also decline with distance even if no other costs of distance are involved.

The arguments are so complex that scholars have tended to use that surrogate for the distance variable which seems intuitively the most appropriate. Thus Linnemann in a study of international trade used route distance as a simple 'proxy variable' for all the distance barriers.[24] On the other hand a large number of gravity studies of motor vehicle traffic have used travelling time as the simplest proxy variable.[25] Finally a few scholars have used simple fares or freight rates on the assumption that they summarise all the distance effects.

In the discussion of the exponent two schools of thought can be identified. The purists argue that the exponent of minus two must be maintained to preserve the analogy. The equation can then be fitted to a data set by using a calibrating constant

$$I_{ij} = G \cdot P_i P_j \cdot d_{ij}^{-2} \qquad (9.7)$$

where G is redefined as a calibrating constant. Then

$$\log I_{ij} = \log G + \log P_i + \log P_j - 2 \log d_{ij} \qquad (9.8)$$

which can then be solved by arithmetic techniques to yield G.

On the other hand it is possible to argue that the exponent for distance also can be empirically derived. This can be achieved by regression analysis of the quantity $(\log I_{ij} - \log P_i - \log P_j)$ on $\log d_{ij}$ to give an equation of the form

$$\log I_{ij} - \log P_i - \log P_j = a - b \log d_{ij} \qquad (9.9)$$

where $a = \log G$

b is the empirically derived exponent.

A large number of studies have followed this second approach and have seen geographical variations in the exponent as being significant features demanding further interpretation and explanation. Haggett, for example, quotes Hagerstrand's suggestion that the lower exponents observed in the United States than in Europe reflect important underlying differences between the two countries.[26] Smith has mapped differences in the exponent as measuring the strength of inter-island links in Hawaii,[27] while O'Sullivan mapped regional differences in the exponent fitted to originating road freight flows in the United Kingdom.[28] He recorded a wide range in exponents ($-1\cdot3$ to $-4\cdot8$) and suggested explanations based on urban–rural contrasts, centre–periphery differences and, as his analysis concerned mixed commodity flows, differences in commodity mix.

Finally it must be noted that in the present author's opinion the gravity equations can seldom be applied with great confidence to aggregated flows. Indeed the type of justifications for its use discussed above explicity refer to single commodities, or at least nearly homo-geneous commodity groups.[29] In passenger studies also it is doubtful if a single gravity equation should be fitted to heterogeneous passenger flows. As a consequence there is need to inquire into interdependence in flow systems. For example, a flow of foodstuffs in one direction may be dependent upon the flow of fertiliser or agricultural machinery in the opposite direction. The importance of this has already been studied in input–output economics, and a possible use of input–output coefficients as constraints in the gravity model is suggested by Wilson.[30]

Pred has suggested that the gravity model has 'very little theoretical substance . . . and it tells nothing about why observed regularities occur. . . and as a consequence leaves one at a loss when discrepancies occur which cannot be accounted for. . . .'[31] Pred suggests indeed that the gravity model leads to an impasse; new theories, and new models to represent them, must be sought. Without taking Pred's extreme view, and noting Wilson's careful defence, it is clear that the status of the concept is not yet beyond dispute.

Intervening Opportunity

In his studies of human migration Stouffer introduced the concept of intervening opportunity which offered an explanation of distance decay without recourse to the friction due to distance. In Stouffer's own words

There is no necessary relation between mobility and distance ... the relation between mobility and distance may be said to depend on an auxiliary relationship which expresses the cumulated (intervening) opportunities as a function of distance ...

and

... the number of persons going a given distance is directly proportional to the number of intervening opportunities at that distance, and inversely proportional to the number of intervening opportunities.[32]

The operational definition of these variables does not raise any acute problems; the most interesting is probably the definition of 'intervening' space. A simple geometrical definition may well be less useful than one based on route mileage, time or total costs of movement. Isard reviews the many applications of Stouffer's concept in migration studies and concludes that they 'do not constitute conclusive evidence of its validity ... or demonstrate that the Stouffer hypothesis is superior to an appropriately modified Stewart–Zipf [gravity type] hypothesis'.[33]

On the other hand the intervening opportunities method has been widely employed in urban transport studies. Part of this use is based upon convenience, for the data requirements are less than for other commonly used methods, but also upon the better fit of this hypothesis to observed data. For example, in a study of Oslo traffic Clark concluded that 'the prediction errors (i.e. predicted minus observed values) of the intervening opportunities model are less than those for the gravity model in every column (zone) except one'.[34]

A logical examination of the concept reveals both its strength and its flaws. The argument that nearer sources are preferred, *ceteris paribus*, is intuitively reasonable, and consistent with least-effort or cost-minimising assumptions about the space economy. On the other hand the blanket statement that 'there is no necessary relationship between mobility and distance' is inconsistent with the analysis of transport demand offered in chapter 2 above. If the demand for transport is derived from the demand for a good or service which is of itself inversely related to price, and if cost is directly related to distance moved, there must be an inverse relation between mobility and distance. The 'success' of the intervening opportunity theory in urban studies may well be due to the fact that the geographical distances are small, and therefore the friction due to distance is insignificant when compared with the absorption due to intervening opportunities.

9.2 THEORIES BASED ON ECONOMICS

It is clear that many of the geographical distribution theories outlined above lack theoretical rigour, and where greater rigour has been introduced it is based upon probability. Economists on the other hand have sought to define the economic bases of flow systems, usually with special reference to international trade, in economic terms. From these studies two types of approach have emerged: those based on equilibrium theory and those based on linear programming.

Equilibrium Interpretations of Flow Systems

Classical international trade theory sought to explain the pattern of trade in terms of comparative advantage. The concept is illustrated

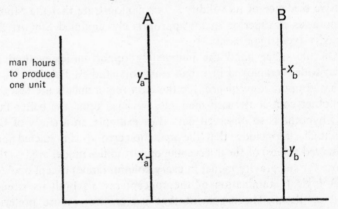

Fig. 9.1. Comparative advantage and the flow of commodities

by a simple two-region economy. If region A and region B both produce two commodities x and y, the costs in man-hours/unit can be specified. In the diagram (figure 9.1) it is clear that, if region A specialises in x only and region B in the production of y only, the same amount of goods can be produced at a lower cost in man-hours. This assumes constant unit costs and zero transport costs between the two regions. Even if transport costs are introduced trade will occur as long as the differences between x_a and x_b are less than those between y_a and y_b.[35]

But it cannot be assumed that the demand for commodity x is fixed; it is therefore necessary to explain the volume of trade between A and B. This can be done in terms of the analysis in section 2.2 above, extended to consider demand and supply curves for each of two regions. Suppose the supply and demand curves are specified in both regions for one commodity (figure 9.2a and b). In the absence of any trade between them, the equilibrium prices can be re-defined as the combined demand of both regions acting on the combined supply (graphically this is achieved by adding the two sets of curves horizontally to produce figure 9.2c). A new equilibrium price is defined in both regions (c_{ab}). It results in a deficit in region A and an equal surplus in region B. This interregionally traded quantity is equivalent to $de = fg$ on the quantity axes. It can be noted that this reduces the price in A and raises the price in B.

The introduction of positive transport costs can be represented by a shift of the curves for the exporting region; in figure 9.2d–f they have been shifted upwards by the amount t. The addition of the curve sets as before leads to a new equilibrium price (c'_{ab}) and once again to a surplus in B and a corresponding deficit in A. The amount interregionally traded is given by $d'e' = f'g'$ on the quantity axes. Finally it can be noted that an increase in transfer costs will lead to a reduction in the quantity traded.[36] These conditions are succinctly summarised by Morrill and Garrison.

Trade will take place between two regions if the difference between regional prices is greater than the amount of transportation costs between them. The amount traded will be that required to shift prices through supply and demand relationships until prices are separated by interregional transportation costs.[37]

This approach was critically examined in the 1920s and 1930s by Heckscher and Ohlin.[38] They argued that the price system is itself a result, not a determinant, of regional specialisation and trade. This effort to redefine the basis of trade resulted in the Heckscher–Ohlin hypothesis which asserts 'that each country will export that

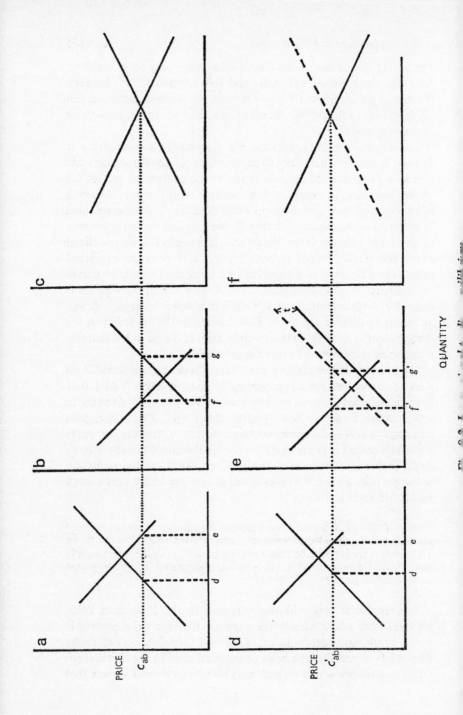

QUANTITY

commodity which is intensive in the use of that country's abundant factor'.[39] Tests of this hypothesis on an international and inter-regional level have proved inconclusive.[40] An examination of Ohlin's original work and of his repeated protestations suggests that the 'Heckscher–Ohlin hypothesis' is not representative of his thought. He wrote 'nothing less than a consideration of all the elements which constitute the price mechanism can adequately explain the nature of interregional trade'.[41] Although this statement has a strong logical base, it poses the almost impossible task of deriving simulta-neously a theory of location and a theory of flow. On the other hand it must be acknowledged that most location theory does imply a pattern of flow. Von Thunen's theory of agricultural location implies a flow of agricultural goods to the central town and of inputs, such as manure, from the town to the farming areas.[42] Similarly central-place theory implies not only a spacing of urban centres, but a movement of goods and people within the urban hierarchy.[43] Finally it can be noted that both agricultural and industrial location theory have acknowledged the presence of differences in factor endowments leading to asymmetry in the distribution of production, and in consequence to flow systems.

Allocation Interpretations of Flow Systems

Work during the second world war on shipping schedules and similar logistic problems led to the emergence of linear programming as a tool for matching a number of supply points to a number of demand points with a minimum use of scarce shipping resources.[44] In simple cases it is usually possible to identify these solutions by simulation and inspection, but linear programming and similar techniques were developed to solve much larger problems. The critical elements in these studies are usually the quantities supplied and demanded, capacity constraints on particular routes or nodes, and the exact specification of the quantity which must be minimised. Table 9.1, for example, shows a simple case solved firstly to minimise ton-mileage and secondly to minimise total costs given certain freight rates. The next stage in the analysis is to introduce non-uniformity in production costs and to specify the joint costs of production and transport as the quantity to be minimised. A study of this type was performed by Henderson for the supply and consumption of coal in fourteen regions within the United States.[45] Similar studies have been performed for commodities as diverse as vegetables in the United States[46] and cement in India.[47] The technique has also been widely used to rationalise inter-plant relations in multi-plant firms.

TABLE 9.1

OPTIMAL FLOW PATTERNS DETERMINED
BY LINEAR PROGRAMMING

Present flows (× 1000 tonnes)

	To	X	Y	Z
From A		3	4	5
B		2	5	5
C		2	4	3
D		5	4	1

Implied transport demand

	X	Y	Z	
A				12
B				12
C				9
D				10
	12	17	14	43

Distance (kilometres)

	X	Y	Z
A	50	70	100
B	90	90	110
C	70	70	70
D	120	90	50

Freight rates
(cents/tonne/kilometre)

	X	Y	Z
A	4	3	2
B	4	3	2
C	4	3	3
D	2	2	2

Costs (cents)

	X	Y	Z
A	200	210	200
B	360	270	220
C	280	210	210
D	240	180	100

Output minimising flow
(× 1000 tonnes)

	X	Y	Z
A	12	—	—
B	—	12	—
C	—	5	4
D	—	—	10

Cost minimising flow
(× 1000 tonnes)

	X	Y	Z
A	12	—	—
B	—	8	4
C	—	9	—
D	—	—	10

Comparisons	*Present flows*	*Minimum output solution*	*Minimum cost solution*
Output (m. tonne/km)	3·80	2·81	2·89
Cost (m. cents)	10·66	8·53	8·33

There remain three questions: firstly whether the technique can truly be extended to encompass all the conditions of real life, secondly whether its assumptions are consistent with reality, and finally whether it provides results which can be tested against reality. The variety of problems to which the technique has been applied suggest considerable flexibility, but two severe problems remain. Firstly it assumes that the functions are linear and thus cannot represent situations in which marked economies of scale are present in production or transport. Secondly the commodity must be relatively homogeneous, or if it is non-homogeneous—for example, wheat and wheat flour—the conversion rates of one commodity to the other must be unequivocal.[48] This homogeneity constraint implies application solely to disaggregated flow systems. A more fundamental criticism is the specification of a quantity to be maximised or minimised in the whole system. In most real situations individuals and companies seek to minimise their own costs or maximise their benefits, not those of the system. The point can be illustrated from the example in table 9.1. For the residents at Y it would be preferable to receive supplies from D (10 000 tonnes), and A or C (7000 tonnes). In both the optimal solutions they receive supplies from B which is their most expensive source of supply. This conflict of interest between the individual and the system has of course far reaching implications. In the present context it raises the question as to whether an optimising solution for a transport system can be considered as a normative explanation of the actual transport flows which are aggregates of individual decisions. In applying linear programming to the system we are facing problems of both criteria and aggregation.

Despite this severe criticism there is room for the use of the technique in explanation. Firstly it can be used to examine the transport flows of centrally controlled economies which have policies determined at the macro-scale. Thus it would seem reasonable to apply linear programming to the distribution of grain surpluses within the USSR. The comparison of the programmed solution with reality would indicate the efficiency of the criteria used in the system, and possibly the presence of intervening factors not explicitly acknowledged by the economic planners. A second similar use would be to examine the transport operations of large organisations, private or public, in the capitalist economies. The activities of the Central

Electricity Generating Board or the National Coal Board in the UK
would be amenable to investigation on these lines. The third application, to the gross flow patterns which are aggregate results of many
individual decisions, may reveal inefficiencies but is unlikely to have
any great explanatory power. Finally, Samuelson has demonstrated
that trade between areas maximises welfare, defined as consumers'
surplus plus producers' surplus.[49] In Beckmann's words, 'It is the
maximisation with respect to commodity flows of total consumers'
plus producers' surplus minus transport costs which may be used as
mathematical equivalent for equilibrium conditions in a spatially
extended market'.[50] The maximisation of this quantity in linear
programming or similar frameworks will define the equilibrium
trading pattern discussed in a preceding section. The third short-
coming is technical; the results are not susceptible to statistical
testing for three reasons: the solutions are unique and there is therefore
no distribution for significance testing, the results for dyads are
interdependent, and the solutions are often unstable. Although
statistical tests such as correlation coefficients are used by some
of the papers quoted, their validity is questionable.[51]

In conclusion, economic studies have emphasised two important
features of flow studies. Firstly, it is clear that the study of flow
systems cannot be carried out in aggregated form; disaggregation
must be carried to the study of individual commodities or closely
related commodity groups. Secondly, the conclusions of economic
analysis are those of Ohlin that ultimate explanation will involve
a simultaneous explanation of both location and flow, although the
use of production and consumption or surplus and deficit figures is
acceptable in short-run studies.

9.3 THEORETICALLY AGNOSTIC APPROACHES

It will be evident that some of the preceding methods, especially the
gravity model, can be used in a theoretically neutral manner as
methods of observing regularities in the phenomena. Such theoretical
agnosticism has been taken a step further in some studies.

A General Systems Approach

A general systems model is a form of functional analysis which
seeks to explain elements of a system by reference to the character

of the system as a whole. In so doing it employs both calibrating constants and empirically derived exponents. Ellis and van Doren used this approach to devise a model for recreational traffic flows in the United States.[52]

For any park j, the flow entering the park is F_j, and

$$F_j = R_k^{-1}P_k \tag{9.10}$$

where P_k is the pressure (end to end) along the link which passes the park (k), and R_k is given by

$$R_k = C \cdot TD_k^b \tag{9.11}$$

where TD_k is the time taken to traverse the link k, and the values of C and b are empirically determined. The solution of these equations proved slightly more accurate than a gravity type model for the same data.

At first sight this method of approach is attractive.[53] It is sufficiently flexible to offer a procedure in widely divergent situations, while the empirical derivation of both the equations and the calibrating constants ensures a high degree of correspondence with reality. These same virtues are also clues to the great weakness of the approach. Its apparent flexibility is due to almost complete theoretical agnosticism, and for this reason no one set of equations has any generality beyond the system for which it was derived. It may however be useful to take this approach further; in a recent critique of gravity models Heggie suggests that empirical studies in large numbers might throw up regularities, such as recurrent forms in the empirically derived equations, which might in turn lead to more fruitful theory.[54] The general systems approach offers a consistent methodology for such empirical work.

A Factor Analytic Approach

Reference has already been made to attempts to identify the major elements in a flow system. There is also a wide literature on classifying areas in formal regions. Berry, who has been active in the application of factor analysis in both these fields, has also suggested that the technique can be extended to define the relation of a flow system to a geographic pattern of formal regions.[55] The essential postulate of his general field theory is 'that the fundamental spatial patterns . . . and the types of spatial behaviour . . . are interdependent and isomorphic'.[56] He proceeds to explore this relation in factor analytic terms in a data set assembled for India.

In the first stage of the analysis 166 descriptive variables were assembled for 325 districts. After preliminary analysis they were reduced to 98 variables which yielded nine factors. Berry interpreted the first five of these respectively as urban–manufacturing regions, irrigation, east and west differences in agriculture, accessibility, and the specialised grain farming of north-west India. The other four factors identified different types of localised mineral production. The results of this analysis were then used in a dimensional analysis, the difference or likeness of regions measured by distances in factor space. These distances were measured not for the original districts but for 36 main regions. As the distance of each region from any other region was measured the total number of such distances was 1260 ($36^2 - 36$). The results for nine factors therefore represented a matrix of 1260×9. In the second stage the flow pattern was represented by a matrix of 1260 dyads (origin–destination pairs) and 63 commodities. A factor analysis of this matrix reduced the original 63 commodities to twelve factors. Each factor had a distinctive commodity mix and in most cases a distinctive spatial structure. Thus the original matrix was reduced to one of 1260×12 in which the cell values were factor scores.

In the third stage Berry sought to correlate the pattern of distances in factor space with the pattern of flows using canonical analysis. He identified four main elements: the exchange of industrial products for agricultural raw materials, exchanges of agricultural specialities between agricultural regions, the intraregional redistribution of agricultural raw materials, and the exchange of industrial specialities between industrialised regions.[57] These results are consistent with *a priori* reasoning, but certain problems remain. In the first place, the type of explanation obtained is no more than a significant statistical association. Secondly, the analysis involves three generalising procedures: the dimensional analysis, the factor analysis of flows and the canonical correlation. In this it runs counter to some well-established principles such as Ullman's claim that complementarity must be not general but specific. Berry's work can therefore be seen as an empirical verification of the claim that spatial patterns and flows are interdependent and isomorphic but not as an elucidation of that interdependence.

9.4 HYBRID EXPLANATIONS

The ideas presented above are not mutually exclusive and a number of scholars have attempted to use hybrid explanations involving more than one of these concepts.

Ullman's Bases for Interaction

Ullman has suggested a hybrid theory of spatial interaction in which he defines three bases of interaction: complementarity, intervening opportunity and transferability.[58] Although the ideas have been widely quoted and indeed hailed by Bunge as a 'substantial innovation', the framework lacks sufficient rigour of definition.[59]

Ullman defined complementarity between two regions as 'demand in one and supply in the other. . . a function of both natural and cultural areal differentiation and of areal differentiation based upon economies of scale'.[60] Unfortunately the word appears to cover three distinct concepts. *Latent complementarity* can be defined in terms of the latent production potential of the resource base. In this sense complementarity is related to the concept of comparative advantage. *Potential complementarity* occurs in a short-run analysis when surpluses and deficits exist. These are the initial conditions of the linear programming transportation problem, and the starting point of gravity and interactance models of the type proposed by Wilson.[61] Thirdly, Smith measured a quantity which is best termed *achieved complementarity*, the degree to which sets of surpluses and deficits have been matched.[62] Both these latter concepts have been discussed in earlier sections.

Ullman borrowed the concept of intervening opportunity from Stouffer[63] but defines it rather differently: 'complementarity will generate interchange between two areas if no intervening source of supply is available'.[64] This is a curious borrowing for two reasons. Firstly Ullman replaces Stouffer's probabilistic use with a deterministic use. Secondly Stouffer used intervening opportunity on the grounds that 'there is no necessary relation between mobility and distance'[65]—an assertion which may be doubted on economic grounds. Ullman uses intervening opportunity but retains the effects of distance in his third basis for interaction: transferability. This also is a hybrid including two distinct concepts, the transferability of the *commodity* and of the intervening *earth space*. Thus a commodity may have a low transferability due to its fragility, its perishability or, borrowing from economic analysis, its price elasticity of demand and supply. The earth space will have varying transferability according both to natural conditions and to the type of transport system installed.[66] Ullman's work re-emphasises a methodological point: that hybrid models must have terms carefully defined in order to avoid ambiguity or duplication. Such error will be easier to detect if the quantities are formally specified. In addition it is clear that where the relation between the elements of a hybrid is unspecified, verbally or formally, the resultant theory is untestable.

A Hybrid System for Traffic Studies

Eliot-Hurst's work on Perth provides an elementary example of a formally structured hybrid.[67] In his study of traffic generation he concluded that of a number of multiple regression models the best predictor was

$$y = C_0 + P(1 + D)^{-2} + E^2(1 + D)^{-2} + V(1 + D)^{-2} + L(1 + D)^{-2}$$
(9.12)

> where y = trips between origin and destination
> D = distance between origin and destination
> P = population at each point
> E = employment at each point
> V = car ownership at each point
> L = land use index for each point
> C_0 is a constant.

In this equation the third term represents a gravity approach, the fifth a land use based approach. The relation between elements of the hybrid is specified as a summation of the independent terms. The form of the equation is suitable for solution by regression analysis, but more complex forms could be handled by a logarithmic transformation before solution. It is hybrid theories of this kind which are most widely used to 'explain' and predict traffic in major urban transport studies.[68]

10 The Intermodal Allocation of Flows

Even a cursory examination of transport systems reveals that they differ greatly in the proportion of traffic allocated to competing modes. Indeed the proportions vary so widely that it is impossible to make any general description of the patterns which result. Studies of the problem have therefore concentrated upon two or three themes: the identification of factors determining the intermodal split, the ranking of these factors in order of importance, and the construction of theories, formalised as working models, which both accurately reflect the decision making process and produce aggregate patterns consistent with reality.

10.1 DETERMINANTS OF INTERMODAL SPLIT IN FREIGHT STUDIES

Previous authors have identified a very large number of supposed determinants of intermodal split. For the purpose of discussion they can best be considered under the headings in figure 10.1.[1] The argument implied is that certain characteristics of the firm and certain characteristics of the consignment together result in objective differences between competing modes. There are however certain behavioural factors—information, ability to use it, perception, and so on—which may lead to a decision which is less than optimal in objective terms. Finally it can be noted that some factors, such as the amount of traffic which the firm generates, may be relevant both to the objective differences and to the behaviour. Furthermore not all the factors listed will be independent. For example the origin and destination regions largely determine the length of haul which together with type of commodity and consignment size will in most cases determine the charges by alternative modes. Similarly the

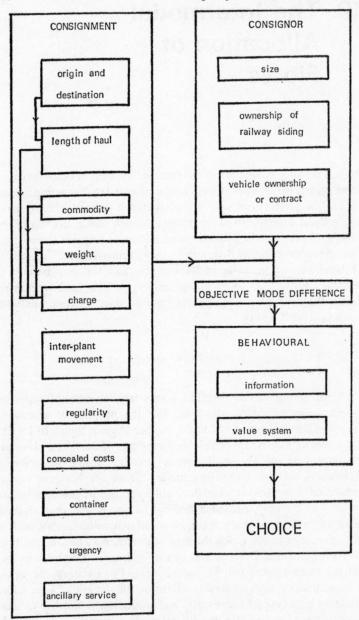

Fig. 10.1. Determinants of intermodal allocation: freight traffic

origin, destination and length of haul will in most cases determine journey times. Most of the factors listed are self-explanatory, but the entry 'ancillary services' is meant to cover those cases where the transporting agent, whether the firm's employee or the transporter's, carries out some ancillary activity of, say, documentation or sales.

Factors relating to the firm constitute a smaller group. Three of them are determinants of intermodal split for a specific consignment, but are more truly seen as results of past intermodal split decisions by the firm. A study of the reasons underlying such decisions in the United Kingdom was made in 1959.[2] Althouth the data collection exercise was inadequate, the results (table 10.1) are instructive and

TABLE 10.1

REASONS FOR RUNNING OWN VEHICLE FLEET
IN PREFERENCE TO USING RAIL TRANSPORT
(4,837 UNITED KINGDOM FIRMS, 1959)

Reasons	*Percentage* (weighted by number of vehicles operated by firm)
Speed of delivery and certainty of timing	75
Cost	56
Placing goods in premises beyond point served by public services	42
Avoidance of breakage or damage	44
Avoidance of pilferage	25
Reduction in packing materials and packing costs	31
Ensuring prompt return of empties	32
Specially constructed vehicles not supplied by public carriers	31
Installation and maintenance services by driver	4
Other special services by driver	32
Advertising on vehicle	32
Other reasons	22

Source: Traders' Road Transport Association. *Survey of C Licensed Vehicles,* London (1959).

justify the inclusion of most of the factors already considered: cost, speed, ancillary services and special vehicles. Clearly the decision about location (on railway lines or sidings), vehicle ownership and contracts represent the firms' long-term decisions about intermodal split; once a firm has so committed itself it will seek to maximise utilisation of the facilities so acquired.

The Relative Importance of Factors

Three methods of assessing the importance of these factors can be used. The first is to collect information on the factors which decision makers themselves are most often conscious of considering. Studies of this type in the United Kingdom have stressed speed (including reliability), loss, theft, damage and costs. A second line of approach is based upon information available. Only if information is available can the factor be considered a likely basis for intermodal split. The results of surveys show a considerable lack of adequate knowledge. The survey by Bayliss and Edwards showed that information on costs by alternative modes was only available for between a quarter and a third of consignments studied.[3] Walters reported that only 17 per cent of firms regularly compared transport costs and 23 per cent of firms had never done so in living memory.[4] A similar result was reported by Walters for damage to consignments; only 8 per cent of the firms surveyed maintained 'records of damage on each form of transport and consider them in making decisions about traffic allocations'.[5] Few firms kept regular records of transit times and delays. This widespread lack of knowledge suggests that decisions are based on the generally accepted view of the vices and virtues of the available modes, not on careful comparison.

The third line of investigation is the objective reality. If a transport manager does make careful comparison between modes, is there evidence that he will discover marked differences between modes? This will differ according to the factor. Differences in rates charged are relatively easily ascertained and the results are usually easily interpreted. On the other hand differences in speed are less easily estimated, unless matched sample consignments are sent for test purposes, and two surveys have suggested that it is not average speed but the incidence of occasional excessive delays which most often shows differences between modes.[6] Similarly the perception of loss and damage appears to be based on the occasional spectacular mishap, rather than on any consistent differences in the records of competing modes.

Modelling Intermodal Split

Faced with so many determinants of intermodal allocation a number of strategies are available for theory building and modelling. The simplest conceptually, but most difficult technically, is to use all recorded variables to predict the allocation of traffic. Such an approach was adopted by Bayliss and Edwards, who used 25 different independent variables to predict allocation to alternative modes.[7] The large number of variables failed to yield a very high correlation coefficient and the proportion attributable to each variable was rather small.

For technical reasons it is desirable to reduce the number of independent variables. It also seems more realistic to suppose a decision maker who considers four or five variables than one who considers a much larger number. The number of variables can be reduced either by elimination or combination. If a variable selected *a priori* is empirically shown to be little considered by decision makers, to be considered on incomplete evidence or to yield little objective difference between competing modes, its elimination from analysis may be justified. Similarly if one variable is shown to be closely correlated with another variable it may be reasonable to omit it from consideration. Finally, if an exhaustive analysis reveals that the variable has negligible explanatory power in the statistical sense, it may be safely rejected. This allows the statistical modelling of theory in much less complex forms and a reduction of the number of terms in the predicting equations.

The same effects can be achieved by the combination of variables. For example, it may be possible to cost the losses due to theft or damage in transit as an insurance premium, as a replacement cost or as a cost of additional safety precautions, such as special packaging. This cost can then be added to the freight rate charge as part of the real cost to the consignor of making the consignment. Similarly it may be possible to impute additional costs, chiefly inventory costs, of slow transit times and occasional delays.[8] Although such a combination of variables is reasonable—indeed it specifies how a decision maker *ought* to behave—one may doubt whether it is an accurate representation of actual behaviour.

The mathematical model most commonly adopted in the study of intermodal split is multivariate correlation and regression. Although it raises some technical problems it can be used to present estimates of explained variation, to measure the relative strength of variables and to produce a parsimonious model, for example, by using stepwise regression. An initial problem is to provide meaningful measures of the qualitative factors, but considerable success has been achieved by using binary variables (score of 1 for presence, 0 for absence). The regression model is most widely used, but other mathematical and statistical models are available. For example Alan Wilson has suggested the extension of his entropy concepts into this field.[9] But whatever method is employed the approach is theoretically agnostic and the various coefficients are always empirically derived.

10.2 DETERMINANTS OF INTERMODAL SPLIT
IN PASSENGER STUDIES

In passenger studies the main focus of attention has been intra-urban movements,[10] but a few studies have also been addressed to inter-urban flows.

Determinants of Modal Choice

The basic list of possible determinants is similar (figure 10.2). It is argued that characteristics of the trip and characteristics of the trip-maker together result in a series of objective differences, and the final decision will also be influenced by behavioural characteristics of the decision maker. The characteristics of the trip include origin and destination, which themselves determine whether a modal choice exists, and the trip length, which largely determines both the out-of-pocket costs and the duration of the trip. The characteristics of the trip maker again include some elements which may reflect long-term intermodal split decisions. For example, residence close to a public service route may imply an earlier commitment to public transport while the absence of car ownership immediately eliminates an important element of choice in the short run. The income variable may operate in a number of ways: by affecting the imputed value of travelling time or the probability of vehicle ownership, and as an indicator of social class, it may be related to the behavioural response to objective differences between available modes. The group of behavioural variables once again includes the existence, accuracy and lack of bias in the information available; it will also

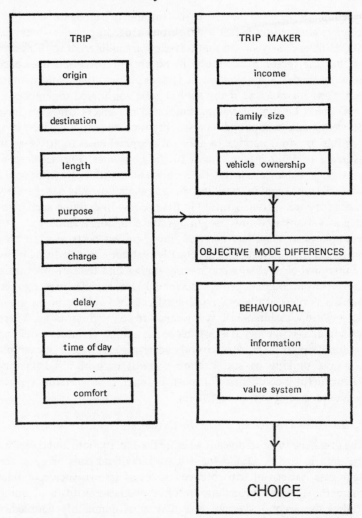

Fig 10.2. Determinants of intermodal allocation: passenger traffic

include differences in the valuation of travelling time, discomfort, and so on. Gronau, for example, demonstrates a strong probability that incomes affect the implicit valuation of travelling time.[11]

Once these variables have been defined it is again desirable to reduce their number for computation; such a reduction may be achieved by elimination, combination or by the use of surrogate variables. *A priori* elimination seems a dangerous procedure, unless previous studies have clearly shown that travellers are indifferent to the factor or that the factor itself results in no real or perceived difference between modes. Combination of factors on the other hand is quite common: for example many studies have considered differences in total time (the sum of waiting times and movement times) or have devised some compound accessibility-time index; similarly it is possible to add a number of different marginal costs to arrive at an estimate of total marginal cost to the consumer. Furthermore, it may be possible to convert time units to cost units by imputing a value for time spent in travelling. Such a calculation may be separately made for each income stratum in the society. In defining such compound variables various weightings are commonly employed. For example most travellers perceive out-of-pocket costs at their true value but tend to discount the equally real but concealed categories of marginal cost. Many commuting studies find that a bus or train fare is fully accounted, petrol costs for a private vehicle are recognised but discounted, while other marginal costs of vehicle operation—depreciation, maintenance, tyre wear—are counted not at all. There are some cases in which it is possible to use a single variable as yielding an approximate measure of several underlying variables. For example a simple ranking by socioeconomic status may be a satisfactory surrogate for income (therefore costs of time), car ownership, type of residence, size of family, and so on.[12]

Modelling Intermodal Choice by Passengers

The first issue to be resolved is whether the explanation, and therefore the data to test it, should focus upon individual trips or upon the aggregate pattern of trips between zones of known socioeconomic characteristics. As these data are often available in town planning studies the second alternative is that most commonly adopted.[13] A second issue, which is often resolved pragmatically, is whether differences between modes should be expressed in absolute or ratio form.

A surprisingly large number of studies have decided that a single difference or ratio gives an adequate explanation of observed patterns. The simplest technique is to plot the proportion of trips using a mode against the time or cost comparison selected. The resulting 'diversion curves' can then be fitted to these observations and the graph used to predict intermodal allocation. If the curves are fitted mathematically the resulting equations can be used for prediction. The technique can be refined by fitting different curves for sub-groups within the population studied. It is difficult to extend the technique to consider more than two competing modes. Finally it is evident that the technique depends upon extrapolation from one situation to another which is assumed to be analogous.[14]

Once again the model most commonly used is regression, in which a number of independent variables are used to predict modal choice. The method yields useful results—percentage of observed variation explained, regression coefficients, and so on[15]—but it has technical problems, and there are methodological problems in the interpretation of observed regression coefficients. Once again too there are alternative approaches such as Wilson's entropy concept,[16] but they have not been fully developed or explored.

As a postscript it must be noted that intermodal split has been one of the areas of active government intervention in the transport sector which will be examined in the next chapter. Such government intervention cannot be ignored when explaining the patterns which exist in a specific case. Conversely this discussion of the determinants of intermodal split reveals the complexity of the decision making process and the problems which face a government in this field.

11 Decision Making and Government Policy in the Transport Sector

The intervention of government in the transport sector may be based on two different though related arguments. The first argument is based upon the quality of private decision making, in terms of the information available, the time scale adopted and the motives of the decision makers. As such it is fundamentally a critique of managerial efficiency in free enterprise systems. The second argument is more fundamental in that it identifies the reasons for intervention in the nature of transport itself. Among these are the 'indirect' nature of transport demand, and the important externalities associated with many aspects of transport which affect the efficiency of the transport sector itself and the economy and society as a whole. This case for government intervention is so strong that governments throughout the world, regardless of ideology, have accepted the need for intervention in the transport sector. In doing so they have developed new forms of project appraisal which are reviewed in the first section of this chapter. The remaining sections concern the provision of network capacity, the provision of public service vehicle capacity and the allocation of traffic to alternative modes.

11.1 CRITERIA FOR GOVERNMENT DECISIONS

The intervention of government in the transport sector is based upon the belief that some aspect of the system could be improved. In most cases there is an added implication that the implementation of the changes will be commercially unprofitable. It is therefore necessary to identify other criteria by which to determine the viability of proposals and to compare the merits of alternative projects. In many cases these decisions are made on the basis of political expediency at least cost, but in recent years new criteria have been developed.

Social Cost–Benefit Analysis

It is acknowledged that most transport decisions have widespread external effects. Some of these effects are beneficial but others are damaging; some are confined to the transport sector but others affect the society as a whole. Social cost–benefit analysis attempts to identify and value some of these effects and to arrive at a net social value for any choice.

The discussion of cost–benefit analysis usually recognises two categories of costs and benefits: commercial and externalities. The first category appears directly in the accounts of the body which implements the decision; it will include capital expenditure, and recurrent revenue and expenditure in operation. Items in the second category are equally 'real' but for a variety of reasons will not appear in that accounting framework. For example, some of the benefits —such as environmental quality—may be intangible, but even where the benefits are tangible and can be valued it may be impossible to devise a method of charging those who receive them. Similarly, some real costs are intangible or, if they are tangible, no fair method of compensation can be devised. Commercial and external categories of costs and benefits are usually termed, together, the efficiency benefits, and most authorities argue that they should be the only categories considered.[1]

Discounted Cash Flow

In this consideration another point must be covered. If a project is designed with an engineering 'life' of twenty years few societies will be indifferent as to when in that period the benefits accrue and the costs are incurred: a simple aggregation of net benefits is therefore unrealistic. The technique known as *discounted cash flow* weights costs and benefits by their incidence in time according to a notional interest or discount rate, to yield the *discounted present value* (DPV) of the investment.

$$\text{DPV} = \sum_{i=0}^{i=n} (B_i - C_i)(1 + r)^{-i} \qquad (11.1)$$

where n is the length of life of the project
  B_i are the benefits in the ith year
  C_i are costs in the ith year
  r is the discount rate.

The equation can be used to estimate DPV for a known discount rate, or indeed for a range of discount rates. Alternatively it may be used to calculate that value of *r* for which the DPV is zero: such a value is termed the *internal rate of return* of the project.[2]

The two categories of costs and the discounting technique can be illustrated from a study made by Foster and Beesley of a proposed extension to the London underground railway system. The summary of the results of that study reveals that if the fare structure could have been designed to charge all those using the line for all the benefits they would receive, the DPV of the project would have been negative. Over half the benefits accrued to travellers on other routes and by other modes due to a reduction in congestion, and it was those benefits which made the project viable in cost–benefit terms. Finally it can be noted that the results were extremely sensitive to the choice of interest rate: with a rate of 4 per cent the DPV was about £64m, but with a rate of 8 per cent it fell to about £13m.[3]

Secondary Benefits

In some situations there is a temptation to include a third category of benefits or costs. In many cases additional benefits are advanced by some group anxious to justify a decision which is not viable under efficiency criteria. In most circumstances too these additional benefits are illusory.[4] Firstly, there are those apparent benefits which on close inspection are seen to be a capitalisation of benefits already assessed: for example, if housing prices rise in the vicinity of a new commuter route, the rise is a capitalisation of reduced fares, time or inconvenience for commuters.[5] Secondly, there are apparent benefits which are in reality multiplier effects of benefits already considered: for example, a new road may result in increased agricultural production. This is the supply schedule adjusting to reduced costs of inputs and lower costs of delivery to market. Thirdly, there are occasions when the effect is to redistribute resources between groups in society or between areas. If the direction of the redistribution is desirable it may be thought a benefit, if undesirable deemed a cost. In his minority conclusion to the report of the Roskill Commission Buchanan argued that airport location at Cublington would involve the development of an urban complex in an undesirable position in terms of regional planning. He believed that this cost was sufficient to reverse the project ranking yielded by conventional cost–benefit analysis.[6]

On the other hand it is often argued that road and bridge construction in depressed regions will lead to a redistribution of employment which is a benefit in regional planning terms. The inclusion of such benefits in cost–benefit analysis is unacceptable unless the original project design specifies joint objectives, such as the solution of a transport problem *and* the redistribution of employment;[7] and redistribution effects of this kind will inevitably imply value judgements of an acute type.[8]

Finally it may be argued that due to multiplier effects or redistribution effects the whole economy becomes more efficient and the project therefore contributes to a growth in GNP. Such an argument again involves double counting if GNP effects are seen as additional benefits. On the other hand there are some communities for which the growth of GNP is seen as the major goal of policy, and some progress has been made towards an alternative form of project assessment. An essential precondition for such an alternative is a working model of the economy which specifies the supply and demand relations for all sectors of the economy. Bos and Koyck have illustrated the possible form of such a scheme based upon the general econometric model proposed by Tinbergen. They consider the effects of major route construction in a simple two-region, three-sector economy with known supply and demand elasticities. The most important finding is that the GNP benefits so assessed considerably exceed the efficiency savings conventionally considered. On the other hand it is clear that the GNP benefits are themselves extremely sensitive to price behaviour in the economy, for example the pricing policy of the transport operators on the new facility. Although such analyses have proved illuminating they are not operational because of the present inadequacies of models and data.[9]

11.2 THE PROVISION OF NETWORK CAPACITY

Underprovision of network capacity can result in serious congestion diseconomies; the expansion of network capacity is relatively slow, and there are important indivisibilities in network provision. These factors combine to encourage government participation in the provision of routes and terminal facilities and to focus the attention on problems of prediction. Accurate prediction is necessary to avoid errors in the amount of capacity provided, in the date at which capacity becomes available and in the order in which projects are completed. It is also necessary if discounting of cash flow is attempted over the capital life of the project. In the aggregate prediction there may be as many as three elements: the overall growth of present traffic, diverted traffic and generated traffic.

In tackling this problem a wide range of techniques have been devised which fall into three main categories: historical prediction, geographical prediction and theoretical prediction.[10] The first category consists of those studies which look at the facility concerned in isolation and attempt to predict its future traffic by extrapolation of a past time-series. Such a study may be based on aggregated or disaggregated flows, for example by direction or commodity. Such an approach cannot include estimates of generated or diverted traffic due to the new facility. It is also inapplicable when the facility is entirely new and not replacing or augmenting any pre-existing facility. The second approach is based on geographical extrapolation from an analogous situation. It is thus useful when a project is entirely new and the traffic will all be generated or diverted. It is not widely used in simple form.[11] The third approach, which is the most common, fits a theoretical model to present flows in order to estimate the traffic generated or diverted by the new facility. For example, if a gravity model is fitted to the present pattern, the reductions in distances or time or costs resulting from the investment can be fed into the equations to estimate diversion and generation.

In reality most studies involve a mixture of these techniques. For example, the aggregate flows in a system may be historically predicted and their allocation between routes and terminals derived from some theoretical model. The Ministry of Transport's study of Portbury, a proposed port complex near Bristol, first predicted the overall growth of shipping inwards and outwards from the United Kingdom, and then used a gravity model to allocate this traffic to ports including Portbury. The gravity model was first fitted to 1964 data and future traffic was allocated according to those parameters.[12] It will be evident that the study ruled out traffic generation: the existence of an additional port is unlikely to affect the tonnage of a major country's international trade. It also ruled out traffic diversion. This would seem to be a serious omission as changes of inland transport, liner trains and motorways especially, will probably reduce the effects of distance for the country in general and for the Bristol region in particular.[13]

A similar approach with a different order is adopted in many studies of new road links. The theoretical model is used to estimate generated traffic; diversion curves are used to estimate diverted traffic and their sum is then projected at a compound rate based on time-series for the region or country as a whole. (Such use of diversion curves is of course a form of geographical extrapolation, as by definition they cannot be known for an as yet unbuilt facility.) This method was applied in a study of England's first major motorway. Traffic was assigned to the motorway on the basis of journey time: if time savings exceeded five minutes the traffic was assigned to the motorway, if time losses exceeded five minutes the traffic remained on its original route; half the trips with intermediate savings or losses were assigned to the motorway. Generated traffic for the motorway was calculated, by reducing the journey-time variable in gravity-type equations, as an additional 10·4 per cent. The sum of these two was then projected at a compound annual rate of 5·4 per cent.[14] The underground railway study referred to in a previous section used similar techniques to predict both diverted and generated traffic.[15]

11.3 THE RURAL TRANSPORT PROBLEM

In the period since 1950 many areas of the United Kingdom have been affected by the reduction of public transport services by road, rail and ferry. Similar problems have been encountered in rural areas in other countries. When this problem is analysed it is seen to be complex. The aggregate demand for transport in rural areas is low and decline in rural population densities further exacerbates the problem. The spatial structure of demand is one of point-to-area and *vice versa*. There are marked diurnal, weekly and seasonal fluctuations in demand. In economic terms the aggregate demand is sensitive to price, partly because of low rural income.[16]

The road network to serve this pattern of demand is usually well established, has a high level of connectivity and allows rapid and cheap vehicle operation at low traffic densities. The recurrent costs of this network are met from general taxation and are often subsidised from outside the problem area. It becomes clear then that the problem is one of vehicle supply. The first element is the distribution of private vehicles. For the wealthier members of the rural community transport has never been better, because the private car is relatively cheap to run and confers a degree of mobility which far exceeds that conferred by rail and bus services at their peak.[17] The second element is the spatiotemporal distribution of public services which are provided for a declining proportion—those too poor to own a vehicle—of a declining population. This residual demand is insufficient to maintain frequent services on a commercial basis.[18]

The rationale for government intervention in this situation may be based on efficiency criteria, welfare criteria or possibly in terms of GNP. The efficiency argument is that there are certain hidden costs, externalities in most cases, of the present trend, and that these outweigh the subsidies which would be necessary to maintain services. For example the withdrawal of public services may increase the transport costs of public health and education undertakings.[19] Secondly there is the argument that the trend represents a reduction in the welfare of a particular group in the community, both socially and geographically, and that this redistribution is contrary to the aims of the society.[20] Finally some protagonists of subsidy argue that it is desirable 'to help preserve a healthy balance of population between rural and urban areas, so that the countryside continues to play an active part in British life, and does not become a series of distressed areas and empty showpieces'.[21] It is, apparently, damaging to the national interest to allow this trend to continue.

Various attempts have been made to solve the problem without recourse to direct subsidy. For example it is often argued that multi-role vehicles could be provided to carry passengers, small freight and postal deliveries. (The carriage of postal traffic might also act as a medium for disguised subsidy.) Although such a solution would marginally reduce the costs attributable to passengers it has already been repeatedly adjudged unlikely to solve the problem except in marginal cases.[22] Another school of thought suggests that different vehicles would have cheaper costs per passenger-mile, for example if minibuses replaced conventional buses. Once again the stratagem would succeed in marginal cases, but no great reduction in unit costs could be expected because many items of cost remain the same, such as drivers' wages.[23]

Another school of thought argues that the hardship imposed is not intolerable and the contraction of services should be allowed to continue. They conclude that intolerable hardship will result in migration (to larger settlements), and that a more rational distribution of population will result. A logical extension of this view is to plan for the relocation of population in larger villages at points easily served by bus services. In reality the current policies seem to allow a progressive withdrawal of services cushioned by occasional subsidy (from government funds) or cross-subsidy (by the operator from more lucrative routes), and it is hoped that the slowed-down withdrawal will allow rural communities to adjust by migration or increased private vehicle ownership and that the problem will 'solve itself'. It shows no sign of doing so.

11.4 INTERMODAL SPLIT AND GOVERNMENT INTERVENTION

The determinants of intermodal split and their role in decision making has already been reviewed. The aggregate pattern of mode and route choice resulting from these decision making processes may have undesirable features—undesirable to society as a whole or to some interest group within it. The result is to provoke interest in the causes of intermodal choice and, in many cases, in the concept of transport coordination.[24] Transport coordination is, in Savage's words, 'much discussed but rarely defined': it would seem to rest on the assumption that, properly viewed, transport forms are complementary and not competitive in nature.[25] This belief is quasi-metaphysical in nature and for this reason the discussions often adopt moral overtones which hinder exact analysis. Further, this same metaphysical quality makes the verification of the basic assumption difficult if not impossible. Finally, it can be noted that there is no good *a priori* reason why technological innovations 'should' be complementary rather than competitive. Nevertheless, a literature has evolved which attempts firstly to identify the criteria on which the complementary roles should be defined, and secondly to suggest mechanisms by which these roles can be established in practice.

'Real Costs'

One definition of coordination focuses upon 'real costs': 'to ensure that the required transport services are provided with the minimum call upon the real resources of the nation',[26] or again by that form of transport whose real economic costs are lowest.[27] This identification of real costs as the kernel of the problem suggests that a simple accounting model will suffice to derive both the criteria and the mechanisms for achieving coordination.

The criteria become least total cost criteria, but the problem lies in the correct identification of the total real costs of all parts of a transport system. One such problem is concerned with the asset value of track. It has long been argued that road transport does not cover the imputed capital costs of roads and bridges: a legacy from the past.[28] A second related problem concerns opportunity costs. If a decision is made to abandon a railway line, opportunity costs are incurred. This problem of opportunity costs is implicit in any marginal cost policy of traffic allocation.

A second problem arises with those costs which though recognised are seldom explicity evaluated. The external diseconomies of congestion, air pollution and traffic noise are recognised social costs of road transport, but only recently have the tools of social cost–benefit analysis been developed to deal with them, and methods of measurement remain uncertain.[29]

The Taxonomic Approach

The taxonomic approach attempts to classify transport demands according to their 'suitability' for a particular transport mode. The Beeching Report on British Railways provides a good example of this approach. It identified nine characteristics of goods traffic to 'determine its relative suitability for road and rail transport': 'the nature of the commodity, loadability, points of origin, terminal conditions, volume and regularity of traffic, average consignment size, geographical location of flows, and length of haul'; '223 million tons of non-railborne traffic were examined to determine their potential suitability for rail haulage'.[30] In the last analysis the principle criteria were that it should be either siding traffic travelling at least 50 miles, or traffic which 'would be carried distances of not less than 70 to 100 miles by liner trains'. In this way 29 million tons of traffic were identified as 'potentially good rail traffic'.[31] Nowhere is this potential 'good' or 'suitability' otherwise defined.

Financial and Fiscal Measures

Where agreement has been reached on the desirable intermodal split it is possible to take fiscal measures which ensure that the consumer costs of transport reflect the allocation of traffic which is most desirable. This is achieved by the direct control of freight rates, or indirectly by heavy taxation and related charges.

The direct control of freight rates is widely practised by West European governments. In Germany, for example, the 'sole purpose of the road tariff was to protect the railway from road haulage competition'.[32] It consisted of a minimum rate applied to all traffic over fifty kilometres. A similar legislative device was used in France, and the attempt to base it on operating costs, thereby claiming to protect road haulage from internal excessive competition, was in Bayliss's opinion a 'facade'.[33] The problem of such an approach lies in enforcement. Even if the cash sums paid reflect the authorised tariff, there is no way of preventing concealed rebates or special peripheral services. It was for this reason that Hazlewood rejected the approach in the East African context.[34]

The attempt to achieve a similar aim by taxation is outlined in the 1967 White Paper,[35] and is vigorously rebutted by Walters.[36] Once again the tax—a heavy increase in licence fees for road hauliers —could be justified on the grounds that heavy vehicles increase both the capital and recurrent cost of road provision. The bluntness of this policy tool is summed up in the Geddes report.

Ideally if the sole purpose of taxation was to alter the distribution of traffic, the taxes imposed should be so designed as to divert the desired volume and types of traffics, without falling on those users whose traffics were not to be diverted; for otherwise the diversion would be achieved not only at the expense (unavoidably) of the traffic to be diverted, but also at the expense (unnecessarily) of the remaining traffic.... The adoption of a selective approach in taxation presupposes that it is known which classes of traffics could more readily be diverted than others or which traffics the authorities wished to have diverted. But if this information were available, direct control... would be as promising a solution...[37]

Physical Controls

Wherever the government has effective control it can control the supply of vehicles or rolling stock, thus creating a shortage. In every case this control has been exercised to limit the activities of the road haulage industry. Such restrictions may be aimed at the total stock within a country, or the capacity available in particular areas or indeed along selected routes. In some cases selectivity will be increased by limiting some classes of operator more severely than others.

In addition the same powers which are used to achieve coordination may be used to prevent 'wasteful competition' within the road haulage industry.

The adoption of this procedure was urged in many countries in the period after the first world war. In Great Britain it became official policy in the Road and Rail Traffic Act of 1933. The principal elements of that act and succeeding legislation of 1947 and 1953 were incorporated in the Road Traffic Act of 1960.[38] This act was based upon a fourfold division of all commercial vehicle licenses. The A licence was limited to public carriers, who might use authorised vehicles for hire or reward. A declaration was required as to the 'normal use', but this was not entirely binding. A second licence was issued to operators who wished to carry under contract for a single customer: it was termed Contract A. The limited carriers or B licence could carry only the owner's goods, and other goods subject to special conditions. These special conditions usually specified 'the type of goods that may be carried, the person for whom goods may be carried, the area of operation, or some combination of all these factors'. The issue of such licences was the function of a licensing authority. The C licence was for the carriage of owner's goods alone. The restrictions on Contract A and C licences were almost entirely directed to maintain safety and other standards, but A and B licences were used to influence transport competition and coordination. All other transport operators were given the right to lodge objections. In addition experience and case law made the 'normal user' provision more binding, and the A and B licences became more alike. The Geddes Report concluded: 'in practice the volume of objection by existing licensed operators and the Railways seems to have made it very difficult for a new entrant to Road to obtain an A licence'.[39] In this way entrance into A and B class haulage was checked; there was some attention to regional provision of capacity, and little control of traffic on specific routes.

In some countries, however, there is an attempt to control traffic on specific routes. In Kenya the Madan Committee recommended trip length restrictions and the identification of controlled routes.[40] These routes were those running parallel to the railway, and for them a severely limited number of special licences was issued. A similar division into local routes and National Main Routes was adopted in Tanzania.

These problems and many others remain of pressing importance in planning, whether that planning is devoted to the increase of national product, the distribution of welfare or the maintenance of environmental quality. Their solution will depend upon accurate description, analysis and explanation of transport activities: a task to which this book has been addressed.

Notes

Some readers may find parts of this work difficult because they are unacquainted with the terminology of economics,[1] mathematics,[2] statistics[3] or the 'new geography'.[4] Some books which will assist them are listed below under 'Background References'. There, too, are listed a number of works in transport geography which cannot be ignored though they receive little reference in the text.[5,6,7,8,9]

If the reader wishes to extend his reading beyond the references given, he will find the periodical literature a rich field. There are a few journals specifically directed to transport studies, including the *Journal of Transport Economics and Policy*, the *Journal of Transport History*, *Traffic Quarterly* and *Transportation Research*. In addition there are reports from the various government research organisations, notably the Transport and Road Research Laboratory in Britain, and the Highway Research Board in the United States. Various professional bodies publish relevant journals, especially the Institute of Transport (London), the Town Planning Institute (UK) and the American Institute of Planners. Among geographical journals four have emerged as principal contributors on transport studies: *Geographical Analysis*, the *Annals of the Association of American Geographers*, *Economic Geography* and the *Canadian Geographer*.

Background References

1. R. G. Lipsey, *An Introduction to Positive Economics*, Weidenfeld and Nicholson, London (1966).
2. R. G. D. Allen, *Basic Mathematics*, Macmillan, London (1962).
3. M. J. Moroney, *Facts from Figures*, Penguin, Harmondsworth (1951).
4. P. Haggett, *Locational Analysis in Human Geography*, Arnold, London (1965).
5. J. H. Appleton, *The Geography of Communications in Great Britain*, Oxford U.P., London (1962).
6. J. E. Becht, *A Geography of Transportation and Business Logistics*, Brown, Dubuque (1970).
7. R. Clozier, *Géographie de la Circulation*, Editions Génin, Paris (1963).
8. P. Haggett and R. J. Chorley, *Network Analysis in Geography*, Arnold, London (1969).
9. E. J. Taaffe and H. L. Gauthier, *Geography of Transportation*, Prentice-Hall, Englewood Cliffs (1973).

References

1 INTRODUCTION

1. R. Hartshorne, The nature of geography, *Annals of the Association of American Geographers*, **29** (1939).
2. A. Hettner, Der gegenwartige Stand der Verkehrsgeographie, *Geographische Zeitschrift*, **3** (1897), p. 626.
3. *Ibid.*
4. A. Huckel, La géographie de la circulation selon Friedrich Ratzel *Annales de Geographie*, **15** (1906), pp. 401–78. In fairness it must be stressed that Huckel saw Ratzel as his main inspiration and rejected the analogy with bloodstream (p. 403).
5. E. Pfohl, *Neues Worterbuch der Franzosichen und Deutschen sprache*, Teil II, Leipzig and Zurich (1911), p. 471. The root word *Verkehr* is common to both Ratzel and Hettner.
6. M. A. Lefèvre, *Principes et Problèmes de Géographie humaine*, Legrand, Brussels (1945).
7. L. I. Vasilievsky, Basic research problems in the geography of transportation of capitalist and underdeveloped countries, *Soviet Geography*, **4** (1964), p. 14.
8. P. R. Crowe, On progress in geography, *Scottish Geographical Magazine*, **54** (1938), p. 14.
9. E. L. Ullman, Transportation geography, in P. E. James and C. F. Jones, *American Geography: Inventory and Prospect*, Syracuse U.P., New York (1954), pp. 310–32.
10. J. H. Appleton, *A Morphological Approach to the Geography of Transport*, University of Hull, Occasional Paper No. 3, Hull (1967).
11. R. Clozier, La géographie de circulation, in G. Chabot *et al.* (eds), *La Géographie française au milieu du XXᵉ siècle*, Baillière, Paris (1957), pp. 175–86, especially p. 181.
12. M. Sorre, *Les Fondements de la Géographie humaine*, tome II, *Les fondements techniques*, Paris, Armand Colin (1948), chapter 6.
13. A. M. O'Connor, *Railways and Development in Uganda*, Oxford U.P., Nairobi (1965).
14. W. L. Garrison and M. E. Marts, *Geographic Impact of Highway Improvement*, University of Washington, Seattle (1958).
15. M. D. I. Chisholm, *Geography and Economics*, Bell, London (1966), p. 7.
16. D. L. Munby, *Transport*, Penguin, Harmondsworth (1968), p. 7.
17. S. Troxel, *Economics of Transport*, Rinehart, New York (1955). This is an outstanding exception to the generalisation. See especially chapters 8, 28 and 29.

18. J. Dupuit, On the measurement of the utility of public works (1844), translated by R. H. Barback in *International Economic Papers* (1952), no. 2, pp. 83–110.

2 TRANSPORT DEMAND

1. R. H. T. Smith, Towards a measure of complementarity, *Economic Geography*, **40** (1964), pp. 1–8.
2. J. H. Appleton, *A Morphological Approach to the Geography of Transport*, University of Hull, Occasional Papers in Geography, No. 3 (1965).
3. H. H. McCarty and J. B. Lindberg, *A Preface to Economic Geography*, Prentice Hall, Englewood Cliffs (1966), chapter 9.
4. E. D. Perle, *The Demand for Transportation: regional commodity studies in the United States*, University of Chicago, Department of Geography Research Paper No. 95 (1964).
5. R. N. Taaffe, *Rail Transportation and the Economic Development of Soviet Central Asia*, University of Chicago, Department of Geography Research Paper No. 64 (1960), pp. 104, 106 and 127.
6. For examples see *Traffic in Towns*, Penguin, Harmondsworth (1964), pp. 52 and 82–3.
7. K. R. Cox, The application of linear programming to geographic problems, *Tijdschrift voor Economische en Sociale Geografie*, **56** (1965), pp. 228–36.
8. D. G. W. Timms, Quantitative techniques in urban social geography, in R. J. Chorley and P. Haggett, *Frontiers in Geographical Teaching*, Methuen, London (1965), pp. 243–7.
9. D. S. Neft, *Statistical Analysis for Areal Distributions*, Regional Science Research Institute, Monograph Series No. 2, Philadelphia (1966).
10. M. J. Bruton, *Introduction to Transportation Planning*, Hutchinson, London (1971).
11. S. L. Edwards and I. R. Gordon, The application of input–output methods to regional forecasting: the British experience, in M. Chisholm (ed.) *Regional Forecasting*, Butterworth, London (1971), pp. 415–30.
12. C. M. Tiebout, Regional and interregional input–output models: an appraisal, *Southern Economic Journal*, **24** (1957), pp. 140–7.
13. Bruton, *op. cit.*, chapter 4.
14. M. R. Bonavia, *The Economics of Transport*, University Press, Cambridge (1957 edition), chapter 1.
15. R. G. Bressler and R. A. King, *Markets, Prices and Interregional Trade*, Wiley, New York (1970), chapter 5.
16. *Report of the Select Committee on Nationalised Industries*, London Transport, volume II, HMSO, London (1965), pp. 395–8.
17. The inverse of this argument is apparently accepted in H. P. White, The movement of export crops in Nigeria, *Tijdschrift voor Economische en Sociale Geografie*, **54** (1963), p. 248.
18. G. Manners, Transport costs, freight rates, and the changing economic geography of iron ore, *Geography*, **52** (1967), pp. 260–79.

19. *Ibid.*, p 276.
20. M. Chisholm, *Geography and Economics*, Bell, London (1966), p. 77.
21. British Railways Board, *The Reshaping of British Railways*, HMSO, London (1963), p. 94.
22. *Ibid.*, p. 25.
23. R. H. T. Smith and A. M. Hay, A theory of the spatial structure of internal trade in underdeveloped countries, *Geographical Analysis*, **1** (1970), pp. 131–6.
24. For a discussion of this point see T. E. Kuhn, The economics of transportation planning in urban areas, in *Transportation Research*, National Bureau of Economic Research and Columbia University Press, New York (1965), pp. 297–326.
25. G. Norstrom, Seasonal variations in the employment of bulk cargo tonnage, *Tijdschrift voor Economische en Sociale Geografie*, **52** (1961), pp. 119–28.
26. B. T. Bayliss, *European Transport*, Mason, London (1965), p. 21.
27. *The Reshaping of British Railways, op.cit.*, part I, p. 15.
28. For seasonal factors in European air transport see S. F. Wheatcroft, *The Economics of European Air Transport*, University Press, Manchester (1956), chapter 4.
29. W. Isard, Transportation development and building cycles, *Quarterly Journal of Economics*, **62** (1948), 202–28.
30. C. D. Campbell, *British Railways in Boom and Depression: an essay in trade fluctuations and their effects, 1918–1930*, King, London (1932).
31. S. Gregory, *Statistical Methods and the Geographer*, Longmans, London (1963), chapter 3.
32. J. D. Coppock, *International Economic Stability*, McGraw-Hill, London (1962), chapters 1 and 2.
33. *Ibid.*, pp. 24–5.
34. J. E. Freund and F. J. Williams, *Modern Business Statistics*, Prentice-Hall, Englewood Cliffs (1958), chapters 17–19.
35. An analysis which complements this discussion (though orientated towards the location of industry) is O. Lindberg, An economic geographical study of the localisation of the Swedish paper industry, *Geografiska Annaler*, **35** (1953), pp. 28–40.
36. W. A. Mackintosh, *Prairie Settlement: the geographical setting*, Macmillan, Toronto (1934), especially chapter 3.
37. P. Hall, *London 2000*, Faber, London (1963).
38. A general account can be found in J. B. Mitchell, *Historical Geography*, English Universities Press, London (1954), chapter 7.
39. D. St J. Thomas, *The Rural Transport Problem*, Dartington Hall studies in rural sociology, Routledge Kegan Paul, London (1963).
40. A. M. Hay, Imports versus local production: a case study from the Nigerian Cement Industry, *Economic Geography*, **47** (1971), pp. 384–8.
41. A. O. Hirschmann, *The Strategy of Economic Development*, Yale U.P., New Haven (1960).

42. For a simple introduction to the concept see M. Chisholm, *Geography and Economics*, Bell, London (1966), pp. 40–4.
43. For an example see J. E. Martin, *Greater London: an industrial geography*, Bell, London (1966), pp. 15–23.

3 ELEMENTARY DESCRIPTION OF TRANSPORT NETWORKS

1. M. Jefferson, The civilising rails, *Economic Geography*, 4 (1929), pp. 217–31.
2. W. Z. Ripley, Geographical limitations of consolidated systems, *American Economic Review*, 14· (1924), supplement, pp. 52–64.
3. P. Hall (ed.), *Von Thunen's Isolated State*, Pergamon, London (1966), p. 7.
4. Jefferson, *op. cit.*
5. M. Beckmann, *Location Theory*, Random House, New York (1968), pp. 83–5.
6. J. R. Borchert, The twin cities urbanised area: past, present, and future, *Geographical Review*, 51 (1961), pp. 47–70.
7. S. Nordbeck, Computing distances in road nets, *Papers and Proceedings of the Regional Science Association*, 12 (1963), pp. 207–20.
8. J. A. Timbers, Route factors in road networks, *Traffic Engineering and Control*, 9 (1967–8), pp. 392–4, 401.
9. A. R. Volk, A method of estimating road mileages, *O & M Bulletin*, 23 (1968), pp. 204–6.
10. M. Madeyski, Transportation network in Poland 1960–61, *Przeglad Komunicakyjny*, 11 (1962), pp. 410–17.
11. A. M. Hay, Connection and orientation in three West African road networks, *Regional Studies*, 5 (1971), pp. 315–19.
12. G. Tornqvist, Transport costs as a location factor for manufacturing industry, *Lund Studies in Geography*, series B, number 23, Lund (1962).
13. Timbers, *op. cit.*, p. 392.
14. Hay, *op. cit.*
15. Timbers, *loc. cit.*
16. E. M. Holroyd, *Theoretical average journey lengths in circular towns with various routeing systems*, Ministry of Transport, Road Research Laboratory Report, no. 43, Crowthorne (1966).
17. Timbers, *op. cit.*, p. 392.
18. Hay, *loc. cit.*
19. D. S. Neft, Some aspects of rail commuting: London, New York, Paris, *Geographical Review*, 49 (1959), pp. 151–63.
20. State of Wisconsin *Blue Book 1968*, Madison, Wisconsin (1968).
21. L. J. King, *Statistical Analysis in Geography*, Prentice-Hall, Englewood Cliffs (1969), pp. 99–102.
22. M. F. Dacey, The spacing of river towns, *Annals of the Association of American Geographers*, 50 (1960), pp. 59–61.
23. King, *op. cit.*, pp. 98–9.
24. E. S. Pearson, Comparison of tests for randomness of points on a line, *Biometrika*, 50 (1963), pp. 315–23.

25. P. J. Rimmer, The problem of comparing and classifying seaports, *Professional Geographer,* **18** (1966), pp. 83–91.
26. D. H. K. Amiran and A. P. Schick, *Geographical Conversion Tables,* International Geographic Union, Zurich (1961).
27. W. H. Wallace, Railroad traffic densities and patterns, *Annals of the Association of American Geographers,* **48** (1958), pp. 352–74.
28. B. J. Turton, British Railway Traffic in 1921, *Transactions of the Institute of British Geographers,* **48** (1969), pp. 155–71.
29. *The Reshaping of British Railways, op. cit.,* part I, pp. 62–77.
30. Turton, *op. cit.*
31. D. E. Christensen, A simplified traffic flow map, *Professional Geographer,* **12** (1962), pp. 21–2.
32. R. E. Carter, A comparative analysis of ports of the United States and their traffic characteristics, *Economic Geography,* **38** (1962), pp. 162–75.
33. Wallace, *op. cit.*
34. W. H. Wallace, Freight traffic functions of Anglo-American railroads, *Annals of the Association of American Geographers,* **53** (1963), pp. 312–31.
35. Turton, *op. cit.*
36. J. N. H. Britton, The external relations of seaports: some new considerations, *Tijdschrift voor Economische en Sociale Geografie,* **56** (1965), pp. 109–12.
37. J. Bird, Traffic to and from British seaports, *Geography,* **54** (1968), pp. 284–302.
38. *Ibid.*
39. P. Haggett, *Locational Analysis in Human Geography,* Arnold, London (1965), pp. 233–6.
40. Carter, *op. cit.*

4 TOPOLOGICAL APPROACHES TO NETWORK FORM

1. W. L. Garrison and D. F. Marble, *The structure of transportation networks,* US Army Transportation Command, Technical Report 62-11, Washington (1962).
2. W. L. Garrison, Connectivity of the Interstate Highway system, *Papers and Proceedings of the Regional Science Association,* **6** (1960), pp. 121–37.
3. K. J. Kansky, *Structure of transportation networks,* University of Chicago, Department of Geography Research Paper no. 84 (1963).
4. *Ibid.,* p. 12.
5. *Ibid.,* pp. 19–22.
6. *Ibid.,* pp. 28–9.
7. C. Werner, Research seminar in theoretical transportation geography in F. Horton (ed.), *Geographic studies of urban transportation and network analysis,* Northwestern University, Studies in Geography, no. 16 (1968), pp. 128–70.
8. *Ibid.,* p. 137.

9. Kansky, *op. cit.*, chapter 3.
10. M. H. Yeates, *An introduction to quantitative analysis in economic geography*, McGraw-Hill, New York (1968), pp. 113–20.
11. P. R. Gould, *Transportation in Ghana*, Northwestern University, Studies in Geography, no. 5 (1960).
12. F. R. Pitts, A graph theoretical approach to historical geography, *Professional Geographer*, 17, 5 (1965), pp. 15–20.
13. Werner, *op. cit.*
14. N. A. Alao, A note on the solution matrix of a network, *Geographical Analysis*, 2 (1970), pp. 83–8.
15. P. Haggett and R. J. Chorley, *Network Analysis in Geography*, Arnold, London (1969), p. 36.
16. Garrison, *op. cit.* (1960).
17. A. Shimbel and W. Katz, A new status index derived from sociometric analysis, *Psychometrika*, 18 (1953), pp. 39–43.
18. Werner, *op. cit.*
19. *Ibid.*, table 3.
20. W. L. Garrison and D. F. Marble, Factor analytic study of the connectivity of a transportation network, *Papers and Proceedings of the Regional Science Association*, 12 (1 964), pp. 231–8.
21. P. R. Gould, On the geographical interpretation of eigenvalues, *Transactions of the Institute of British Geographers*, 42 (1967), pp. 53–86.
22. K. J. Tinkler, The physical interpretation of eigenfunctions of dichotomous matrices, *Transactions of the Institute of British Geographers*, 55 (1972), pp. 17–46.
23. *Ibid.*, p. 28.
24. E. F. Gauthier, Transportation and the growth of the São Paulo economy, *Journal of Regional Science*, 8 (1968), pp. 77–94.
25. K. J. Tinkler, Bounded planar networks: a theory of radial structures, *Geographical Analysis*, 4 (1972), 5–33.

5 THE EXPLANATION OF NETWORK FORM

1. A. C. O'Dell and P. S. Richards, *Railways and Geography*, Hutchinson, London (1971), chapter 3.
2. J. H. Appleton, *The Geography of Communications in Great Britain*, Oxford U.P., London (1962), chapters 1–4.
3. J. H. Bird, *Seaports and Seaport Terminals*, Hutchinson, London (1971).
4. L. T. C. Rolt, *Navigable Waterways*, Longmans, London (1969), pp. 63–5.
5. A. M. O'Connor, *Railways and Development in Uganda*, East African Studies No. 18, Oxford University Press, Nairobi (1965).
6. L. E. Klimm, Man's ports and channels, in W. L. Thomas (ed.), *Man's Role in Changing the Face of the Earth*, University of Chicago Press, Chicago (1956), pp. 535–8.
7. J. E. Vance, The Oregon trail and the Union Pacific Railroad, *Annals of the Association of American Geographers*, 51 (1961), pp. 357–79.

8. D. W. Meinig, A comparative historical geography of town railnets: Columbia basin and South Australia, *Annals of the Association of American Geographers*, **52** (1962), pp. 394–413.
9. H. J. Dyos, Railways and housing in Victorian London, *Journal of Transport History*, **2** (1955), p. 97.
10. S. B. Jones, The 49th parallel and the Great Plains, *Journal of Geography*, **31** (1932), pp. 357–68.
11. K. R. Sealy, *The Geography of Air Transport*, revised edition, Hutchinson, London (1966), p. 116.
12. R. I. Wolfe, *Transportation and Politics*, Van Nostrand, Princeton (1963), pp. 184–5.
13. W. R. Siddall, Railroad gauges and spatial interaction, *Geographical Review*, **59** (1969), pp. 29–57.
14. Appleton, *op. cit.*, p. 158.
15. This example was suggested by E. L. Ullman.
16. A. M. Wellington, *The Economic Theory of the Location of Railways*, Wiley, New York (1887).
17. P. Haggett, *Locational Analysis in Human Geography*, Arnold, London (1965), p. 62.
18. A. Losch, *Economics of Location*, Yale University Press, New Haven (1954), pp. 184–7.
19. C. Werner, The law of refraction in transport geography: its multivariate extension, *Canadian Geographer*, **12** (1968), pp. 28–40.
20. R. Domanski, Remarks on simultaneous and anisotropic models of transportation networks, *Papers and Proceedings of the Regional Science Association*, **19** (1967), pp. 223–8.
21. W. Bunge, *Theoretical Geography*, Lund Studies in Geography, series C, no. 1, pp. 127–8.
22. Werner, *op. cit.*, p. 29.
23. Sealy, *op. cit.*, chapter 8, and *idem*, Stansted and airport planning, *Geographical Journal*, **133** (1967), pp. 350–3.
24. *Commission on the Third London Airport*, Papers and Proceedings, HMSO, London (1970), volumes 7 and 8.
25. J. Adams, Westminster: the fourth London Airport? *Area*, no. 2 (1970), pp. 1–9.
26. K. R. Sealy, The siting and development of British airports, *Geographical Journal*, **133** (1967), pp. 148–77.
27. Bird, *op. cit.*, chapters 8 and 9.
28. This argument is equivalent to the 'spatial margins of profitability' expounded by E. M. Rawstrom, Three principles of industrial location, *Transactions of the Institute of British Geographers*, **25** (1958), pp. 132–42.
29. M. Beckmann, Principles of optimum location for transportation networks, in W. L. Garrison and D. F. Marble (ed.), *Quantitative Geography*, part I, Northwestern University Studies in Geography, no. 13 (1967), pp. 95–119.
30. P. R. Gould, Space searching procedures in geography and the social

sciences, University of Hawaii, Social Science Research Institute Papers, 1 (1966).
31. J. Von Neumann and O. Morgenstern, *Theory of Games and Economic Behaviour*, Princeton U.P. (1944).
32. W. Isard and T. E. Smith, Location games: with applications to classic location problems, *Papers and Proceedings of the Regional Science Association*, 19 (1967), pp. 60–5.
33. M. Austin, T. E. Smith and J. Wolpert, The implementation of controversial facility complex programs, *Geographical Analysis*, 2 (1970), pp. 315–29.
34. Haggett, *op. cit.*, p. 79.
35. K. J. Kansky, *Structure of transportation networks: relationships between network geometry and regional characteristics*, University of Chicago, Department of Geography, Research Paper no. 84 (1963), chapters 3–5.
36. *Ibid.*, p. 52.
37. *Ibid.*, chapter 4.
38. E. J. Taaffe, R. L. Morrill and P. R. Gould, Transport expansion in underdeveloped countries, *Geographical Review*, 53 (1963), pp. 503–29.
39. E. N. Thomas, Maps of residuals from regression, in B. J. L. Berry and D. F. Marble (ed.), *Spatial Analysis*, Prentice-Hall, Englewood Cliffs (1968), pp. 326–52.
40. Kansky, *op. cit.*, chapter 5.
41. J. R. Borchert, The twin cities urbanised area: past, present and future, *Geographical Review*, 51 (1961), pp. 47–70.
42. Kansky, *op. cit.*, chapter 8.
43. *Op. cit.*, p. 138.
44. J. Kolars and H. J. Malin, Population and accessibility: an analysis of Turkish railroads, *Geographical Review*, 60 (1970), pp. 229–46.
45. Taaffe, Morrill and Gould, *op. cit.*
46. A. F. Burghardt, The origins and development of the road network of the Niagara Peninsula, Ontario, 1770–1851, *Annals of the Association of American Geographers*, 59 (1969), pp. 417–40.
47. P. J. Rimmer, The search for spatial regularities in the development of Australian seaports, 1861–96, *Geografiska Annaler*, 49B (1967), pp. 42–54; and The changing status of New Zealand seaports, 1853–1960, *Annals of the Association of American Geographers*, 57 (1967), pp. 88–100.
48. B. Ogundana, Patterns and problems of seaport evolution in Nigeria, in B. S. Hoyle and D. Hilling (eds.), *Seaports and Development in Tropical Africa*, Macmillan, London (1970), chapter 10.
49. R. Lachene, Networks and the location of economic activities, *Papers of the Regional Science Association*, 14 (1965), pp. 183–96.
50. Losch, *op. cit.*, pp. 124–30.
51. R. L. Morrill, *Migration and the spread and growth of urban settlement*, Lund Studies in Geography, Series B, no. 26 (1965).

52. *Ibid.*, pp. 182–3.
53. Kansky, *op. cit.*, p. 126.
54. E. G. Moore and L. A. Brown, Diffusion research in geography: a perspective, *Progress in Geography*, **1** (1969), pp. 128 and 129.

6 TECHNICAL AND ECONOMIC PROPERTIES OF TRANSPORT
   NETWORKS

1. A. C. O'Dell and P. S. Richards, *Railways and Geography*, Hutchinson, London (1971), chapters 5–6.
2. E. L. Ullman, The railroad pattern of the United States, *Geographical Review*, **39** (1949), pp. 242–56.
3. W. R. Siddall, Railroad gauges and spatial interaction, *Geographical Review*, **59** (1969), pp. 29–57.
4. W. L. Garrison, The spatial structure of the economy, *Annals of the Association of American Geographers*, **50** (1960), p. 360.
5. Ministry of Transport, Portbury. *Reasons for the Minister's decision not to authorise the construction of a new dock at Portbury, Bristol*, HMSO, London (1966).
6. R. N. Taaffe, *Rail Transportation and the Economic Development of Soviet Central Asia*, University of Chicago, Department of Geography, Research Paper no. 64 (1960), chapter 4.
7. Ullman, *op. cit.*
8. As reported in *The Economist* (29 July 1967), pp. 420–1.
9. R. E. H. Mellor, Narrow gauge railways in Russia's virgin lands, *Geography*, **40** (1955), pp. 191–2.
10. C. Gerondeau, *Les Transports urbains*, Presses Universitaires de France, Paris (1969), p. 44.
11. R. M. Soberman, *Transport Technology in Developing Countries*, MIT Press, Cambridge (1966), p. 56.
12. A. A. Adedeji, *A Study of Highway Development in the Western Region of Nigeria*, Government of Western Nigeria, Ibadan (1960), p. 34.
13. Soberman, *loc. cit.*
14. Highway Research Board. *Line Haul Trucking Costs in relation to Vehicle Gross Weights*, National Academy of Sciences, National Research Council, Washington DC (1961).
15. D. S. Lawrence, Airports again: access or avoidance? *Traffic Quarterly*, **24** (1970), pp. 10–11.
16. P.-D. Cot, *Les Aéroports*, Presses Universitaires de France, Paris (1963), p. 44.
17. J. G. Ody, Application of cost–benefit analysis to airports: the case of Nicosia, Cyprus, *Journal of Transport Economics and Policy*, **3** (1969), pp. 323–32.
18. Federation of Nigeria, *National Development Plan 1962–8*, Lagos (n.d.), p. 72.
19. University of Lancaster, Department of Operational Research. *UK Deep Sea Trade Routes*, report prepared for the National Ports Council (1967).

20. J. Bird, *Seaports and Seaport Terminals*, Hutchinson, London (1971) chapter 1.
21. *The Reshaping of British Railways, op. cit.*, part I, p. 25.
22. *Ibid.*, pp. 42–4.
23. *Ibid.*, p. 45.
24. M. Beckmann, C. B. McGuire and C. B. Winsten, *Studies in the Economics of Transportation*, Yale U.P., New Haven (1966), pp. 113–17.
25. A. M. Hay, Crop marketing boards and transport policy in Nigeria, 1950–64, *Journal of Transport Economics and Policy*, 4 (1970), pp. 175–7.
26. O'Dell and Richards, *op. cit.*, chapter 3.
27. J. M. Thomson *et al.*, *Motorways in London*, Duckworth, London (1969), chapter 5.
28. Soberman, *op. cit.*, chapter 2.
29. F. S. Campbell (ed.), *Port Dues, Charges and Accommodation, 1969/70*, Philip, London (1969).
30. G. J. Roth, *Paying for Roads*, Penguin, Harmondsworth (1967), chapter 5.
31. W. A. Lewis, *Overhead Costs*, Allen and Unwin, London (1949), chapter 2.
32. A. Melamid, The geography of the Nigerian Petroleum industry, *Economic Geography*, 44 (1968), pp. 37–56, includes an example of this.
33. O'Dell and Richards, *op. cit.*, pp. 45–6.
34. *The Reshaping of British Railways, op. cit.*, p. 6.
35. British Railways Board, *The Development of Major Trunk Routes*, London (1965), appendix A.
36. O'Dell and Richards, *op. cit.*, chapter 4.
37. Highway Research Board, *op. cit.*, pp. 109–11.
38. R. S. P. Bonney and N. F. Stevens, *Vehicle Operating Costs on Bituminous, Gravel, and Earth Roads in East and Central Africa*, Road Research Laboratory Technical Paper no. 75, HMSO, London (1967).
39. E.g. P.-D. Cot, *op. cit.*
40. K. R. Sealy, *The Geography of Air Transport*, Hutchinson, London (1952), chapter 2.
41. Lewis, *op. cit.*, p. 16.
42. *Ibid.*, p. 19.
43. For example, see C. Leubuscher, *The West African Shipping Trade, 1909–1959*, Sythoff, Leyden (1963).
44. L. Cartou, *Le Droit aérien*, Presses Universitaires de France, Paris (1962), pp. 46–8.
45. Leubuscher, *op. cit.*
46. For background see R. O. Goss, *Studies in Maritime Economics*, Cambridge U.P., Cambridge (1968), chapter 2.
47. R. H. T. Smith, *Commodity Movements in Southern New South Wales*, Department of Geography, Australian National University, Canberra (1962), mimeo.

48. J. W. Alexander, S. E. Brown and R. E. Dahlberg, Freight rates, selected aspects of uniform and nodal regions, *Economic Geography*, **34** (1958), pp. 1–18.

7 VEHICLE SUPPLY

1. G. Alexandersson and G. Norstrom, *World Shipping*, Wiley, New York (1963).
2. S. G. Sturmey, *British Shipping and World Competition*, Athlone, London (1962), chapter 9.
3. E. R. Johnson and T. W. van Metre, *Principles of Railroad Transportation*, Appleton, New York (1918), pp. 174–6, and M. Beckman, C. B. McGuire and C. B. Winsten, *Studies in the Economics of Transportation*, Yale U.P., New Haven (1956), chapter 12.
4. J. C. Tanner, Car and motor cycle ownership in the countries of Great Britain, *Journal of the Royal Statistical Society*, series A, **126** (1963), pp. 276–84.
5. A. Cliff and K. Ord, A regression approach to univariate spatial forecasting, in M. Chisholm (ed.), *Regional Forecasting*, Butterworth, London (1970), pp. 47–70.
6. W. A. Lewis, The interrelations of shipping freights, reprinted in *Overhead Costs*, Allen and Unwin, London (1949), chapter 4.
7. N. Ginsburg, *Atlas of Economic Development*, University of Chicago, Chicago (1961), pp. 74–7.
8. W. W. Rostow, *The Stages of Economic Growth*, Cambridge U.P. (1960), chapter 6.
9. W. Owen, *Strategy for Mobility*, Brookings Institution, Washington (1964), chapter 1.
10. A. Silberston, Automobile use and the standard of living, *Journal of Transport Economics and Policy*, **4** (1970), pp. 3–14.
11. J. F. Sleeman, The geographical distribution of motor cars in Great Britain, *Scottish Journal of Political Economy*, **8** (1961), pp. 71–81.
12. Tanner, *op. cit.*
13. B. V. Wagle, A statistical analysis of car ownership in Great Britain and a forecast for 1975, *Journal of the Institute of Petroleum*, **54** (1968), pp. 44–9.
14. T. Hagerstrand, *The Propagation of Innovation Waves*, Lund Studies in Geography, series B, no. 4 (1952).
15. R. Ajo. *An analysis of automobile frequencies in a human geographic continuum*, Lund Studies in Geography, series B, no. 15 (1955).
16. P. Scott, Car ownership in Australian cities, *Town Planning Review*, **31** (1960–1), pp. 125–34.
17. P. Shuldiner and W. Oi, *Analysis of Urban Travel Demands*, Northwestern U.P., Evanston (1962), p. 234.
18. Scott, *op. cit.*
19. J. B. Lansing and G. Hendricks, *Automobile Ownership and Residential Density*, Survey Research Centre, Institute for Social Research, University of Michigan, Ann Arbor (1967), p. 18.

20. J. Forbes, Mapping accessibility, _Scottish Geographical Magazine_, **80** (1964), pp. 12–21.
21. G. A. James, A. D. Cliff, P. Haggett and J. K. Ord, Some discrete distributions for graphs with application to regional transport networks, _Geografiska Annaler_, series B, **52** (1970), pp. 14–21.
22. J. K. Ord, On a system of discrete distributions, _Biometrika_, **54** (1967), pp. 649–56.
23. As reported by Haggett in R. J. Chorley and P. Haggett, _Models in Geography_, Methuen, London (1967), pp. 640–2.
24. W. E. Reed, Indirect connectivity and the measurement of urban dominance, _Annals of the Association of American Geographers_, **60** (1970), pp. 770–85.
25. _Ibid._
26. J. D. Nystuen and M. F. Dacey, A graph theory interpretation of nodal regions, _Papers and Proceedings of the Regional Science Association_, **7** (1961), pp. 29–42.
27. F. H. W. Green, Urban hinterlands in England and Wales: an analysis of bus services, _Geographical Journal_, **96** (1950), pp. 64–81.
28. S. Godlund, _Bus Services in Sweden_, Lund Studies in Geography, series B, no. 17 (1956).
29. D. E. Snyder, Commercial passenger linkages and the metropolitan nodality of Montevideo, _Economic Geography_, **38** (1962), pp. 95–112.
30. Reed, _op. cit._
31. Haggett, _op. cit._, pp. 640–2.
32. W. Christaller, _Central Places in Southern Germany_, Prentice-Hall, Englewood Cliffs (1966), pp. 72–7.
33. K. R. Sealy, _Geography of Air Transport_, Hutchinson, London (1966), p. 112.
34. G. C. Dickinson, Buses and people: population distribution and services in East Yorkshire, _Town Planning Review_, **31** (1960–1), pp. 301–14, and R. J. Johnston, An index of accessibility and its use in the study of bus services and settlement patterns, _Tijdschrift voor Economische en Sociale Geographie_, **57** (1966), pp. 33–8.
35. See for example the references to Sealy and Dickinson above.
36. A. Wren, _Computers in Transport Planning and Operation_, Allan, London (1971), chapter 5.
37. J. Hibbs, _Transport for Passengers_, IEA, London (1963), chapter 4.
38. S. B. Richmond, _Regulation and Competition in Air Transportation_ Columbia U.P. (1961).
39. S. Wheatcroft, _Air Transport Policy_, Michael Joseph, London (1964), chapters 3 and 4.

8 PATTERNS OF TRANSPORT FLOW

1. F. J. Monkhouse and H. R. Wilkinson, _Maps and Diagrams_, second edition, Methuen, London (1964), pp. 254–6.
2. A useful introductory account which touches on many themes in this chapter is given by J. W. Alexander, International trade:

selected types of world regions, *Economic Geography*, **36** (1960), pp. 95–115.

3. E. Thorbecke, European economic integration and the patterns of world trade, *American Economic Association Papers*, **53** (1963), pp. 147–74, and M. Kaser, *COMECON: integration problems of the planned economies*, Oxford University Press, London (1967).

4. G. G. Weigend, Some elements in the study of port geography, *Geographical Review*, **48** (1958), pp. 185–200.

5. E. van Cleef, Hinterland and Umland, *Geographical Review*, **31** (1941), pp. 308–11.

6. J. Bird, Traffic flows to and from British seaports, *Geography*, **54** (1969), pp. 284–302.

7. K. Polanyi, with A. Rotstein, *Dahomey and the Slave Trade—an analysis of an archaic economy*, University of Washington Press, Seattle (1966).

8. J. E. Vance, *The Merchant's World: the geography of wholesaling*, Prentice-Hall, Englewood Cliffs (1970), chapter 7.

9. P. Haggett, *Locational Analysis Human Geography*, Arnold, London (1965), pp. 34–5.

10. I. R. Savage and K. W. Deutsch, A statistical model of the gross analysis of transaction flows, *Econometrica*, **28** (1960), pp. 551–72.

11. S. J. Brams, Transaction flows in the international system, *American Political Science Review*, **60** (1960), pp. 880–98.

12. R. H. T. Smith, *Interregional trade as a component of national unity*, presented to the 21st International Geographical Congress, New Delhi (1968).

13. L. J. King, *Statistical Analysis in Geography*, Prentice-Hall, Englewood Cliffs (1969), chapters 7 and 8.

14. The classification of origins by destinations and *vice versa* could of course be approached by less sophisticated classificatory techniques, e.g. Alexander, *op. cit.*, p. 103.

15. B. J. L. Berry *et al.*, *Essays on Commodity Flows and the Spatial Structure of the Indian Economy*, University of Chicago, Department of Geography, Research Paper no. 111 (1966), essay I.

16. J. D. Nystuen and M. F. Dacey, A graph theory interpretation of nodal regions, *Papers and Proceedings of the Regional Science Association*, **7** (1961), pp. 25–42.

17. A. M. Hay and R. H. T. Smith, *Interregional Trade and Money Flows in Nigeria, 1964*, Oxford U.P., Ibadan (1970), chapter 4.

18. E. L. Ullman, The role of transportation and bases for interaction, in W. L. Thomas (ed.), *Man's Role in Changing the Face of the Earth*, University of Chicago Press (1956), pp. 862–80.

19. Berry, *op. cit.*, p. 237.

20. R. H. T. Smith and A. M. Hay, A theory of the spatial structure of internal trade in underdeveloped countries, *Geographical Analysis*, **1** (1969), pp. 121–36.

21. S. O. Onakomaiya, *The Spatial Structure of Trade in Internal Foodstuffs in Nigeria*, PhD thesis, University of Wisconsin, Madison (1970).
22. The starting point for much of this literature is R. B. Mitchell and C. Rapkin, *Urban Traffic: a Function of Land Use*, Columbia U.P., New York (1954).
23. A. G. Wilson, Interregional commodity flows: entropy maximising approaches, *Geographical Analysis*, **2** (1970), pp. 255–82.
24. L. P. Cummings, *Resid: a computer programme for standardising flows in networks*, University of Iowa, Department of Geography, Discussion Paper no. 14 (1970).
25. R. H. T. Smith, Concepts and methods in commodity flow analysis, *Economic Geography*, **46** (1970), p. 407.
26. R. H. T. Smith, Towards a measure of complementarity, *Economic Geography*, **40** (1964), pp. 1–8.

9 THE EXPLANATION OF FLOW SYSTEMS

1. L. D. Stamp, *Applied Geography*, Penguin, Harmondsworth (1960).
2. F. H. Thomas, Some relationships between a railroad and its region, *Tijdschrift Voor Economische en Sociale Geografie*, **59** (1968), pp. 155–61.
3. D. N. M. Starkie, *Traffic and Industry: a study of traffic generation and spatial interaction*, London School of Economics and Political Science, Geographical Paper no. 3 (1967).
4. *Ibid.*, p. 34.
5. *Ibid.*, pp. 34–6.
6. M. E. Eliot-Hurst, An approach to the study of non-residential land use traffic generation, *Annals of the Association of American Geographers*, **60** (1970), pp. 153–73.
7. M. B. Hesse, *Forces and Fields*, Nelson, London (1961).
8. G. Olsson, *Distance and Human Interaction*, Regional Science Research Institute, Bibliography Series no. 2, Philadelphia (1965), pp. 43–63.
9. See for example M. Schneider, Gravity models and trip distribution theory, *Papers and Proceedings of the Regional Science Association*, **5** (1959), pp. 51–8, and B. Harris, A note on the probability of interaction at a distance, *Journal of Regional Science*, **5** (1964), pp. 31–5.
10. J. D. Carroll and H. B. Bevis, Predicting local travel in urban regions, *Papers and Proceedings of the Regional Science Association*, **3** (1957), pp. 183–97.
11. A. G. Wilson, Interregional commodity flows: entropy maximising approaches, *Geographical Analysis*, **2** (1970), pp. 255–82.
12. *Ibid.*, p. 269.
13. J. H. Niedercorn, and B. V. Bechdolt, An economic derivation of the 'Gravity Law' of spatial interaction, *Journal of Regional Science*, **9** (1969), pp. 273–81.
14. J. Q. Stewart, An inverse distance variation for certain social influences, *Science*, **93** (1941), pp. 89–90.

15. D. A. Smith, Interaction within a fragmented state, *Economic Geography*, **39** (1963), pp. 234–44.
16. E. J. Taaffe, Trends in airline passenger traffic: a geographic case study, *Annals of the Association of American Geographers*, **49** (1959), pp. 393–408.
17. A. M. Voorhees, Discussion: geography of price and spatial inter-action, *Papers and Proceedings of the Regional Science Association*, **3** (1957), pp. 130–3.
18. A. M. Voorhees, A general theory of traffic movement, *Proceedings of the Institute of Traffic Engineers* (1955), pp. 46–56.
19. Wilson, *op. cit.*
20. *Ibid.*, p. 258.
21. R. Gronau, *The Value of Time in Passenger Transportation: the demand for air travel*, National Bureau of Economic Research, Occasional Paper 109, New York (1970).
22. M. Beckmann, C. B. McGuire and C. B. Winsten, *Studies in the Economics of Transportation*, Yale U.P. for Cowles Commission, New Haven (1956), pp. 113–17.
23. W. Beckerman, Distance and the pattern of intra-European trade, *Review of Economics and Statistics*, **28** (1956), pp. 31–40.
24. H. Linnemann, *An Econometric Study of International Trade Flows*, North Holland Publishing Company, Amsterdam (1966), p. 29.
25. Department of Scientific and Industrial Research, Road Research Laboratory, *The London–Birmingham Motorway*, Road Research Technical Paper no. 46, HMSO, London (1960), p. 59.
26. P. Haggett, *Locational Analysis in Human Geography*, Arnold, London (1965), p. 36.
27. D. A. Smith, *op. cit.*
28. P. M. O'Sullivan, Variations in distance friction in Great Britain, *Area*, no. 2 (1970), pp. 36–9.
29. O'Sullivan (*op. cit.*) erroneously uses Wilson's argument as justification.
30. Wilson, *op. cit.*
31. A. Pred, *Behavior and Location, Part I*, Lund Studies in Geography, series B, Human Geography, no. 27 (1967), pp. 111–12, quoting D. Huff.
32. S. A. Stouffer, Intervening opportunities: a theory relating mobility to distance, *American Sociological Review*, **5** (1940), p. 846.
33. W. Isard *et al.*, *Methods of Regional Analysis: an introduction to regional science*, Wiley, New York, p. 541.
34. C. Clark, Trip distribution in Oslo, *Traffic Quarterly*, **22** (1968), pp. 259–70.
35. M. Chisholm, *Geography and Economics*, Bell, London (1966), pp. 40–4.
36. R. G. Bressler and R. A. King, *Markets, Prices and Interregional Trade*, Wiley, New York (1970), chapter 5.
37. W. L. Garrison and R. L. Morrill, Projection of interregional patterns of trade in wheat and flour, *Economic Geography*, **36** (1960), p. 118.

38. B. Ohlin, *Interregional and International Trade*, Harvard U.P. (1933).
39. This phrasing is taken from J. Bhagwati, *International Trade*, Penguin, Harmondsworth (1969), p. 9.
40. See for example W. W. Leontief, *Input–Output Economics*, Oxford U.P. (1966), chapter 5.
41. Ohlin, *op. cit.*, p. 19.
42. Bressler and King, *op. cit.*, pp. 246–7.
43. See for example J. E. Vance, *The Merchant's World: the geography of wholesaling*, Prentice-Hall, Englewood Cliffs (1970), chapter 1.
44. For an introduction to these techniques see S. Vajda, *An Introduction to Linear Programming and the Theory of Games*, Science Paperbacks, London (1966); K. R. Cox, The application of linear programming to geographic problems, *Tidjschrift voor Economische en Sociale Geografie*, **56** (1965), pp. 228–36.
45. J. M. Henderson, *The Efficiency of the Coal Industry: an application of linear programming*, Harvard U.P. (1958).
46. T. E. Tramel and A. D. Seale, Reactive programming of supply and demand relations—applications to fresh vegetables, *Journal of Farm Economics*, **41** (1959), pp. 1012–22.
47. A. Ghosh, *Efficiency in Location and Interregional Flows*, North Holland Publishing Company, Amsterdam (1965).
48. Garrison and Morrill, *op. cit.*, p. 121.
49. P. A. Samuelson, Spatial price equilibrium and linear programming, *American Economic Review*, **42** (1952), pp. 283–303.
50. M. Beckmann, *Location Theory*, Random House, New York (1968), p. 92.
51. Cox, *op. cit.*
52. J. B. Ellis and C. S. van Doren, A comparative evaluation of gravity and system theory models for statewide recreational traffic flows, *Journal of Regional Science*, **6** (1966), pp. 57–70.
53. D. Harvey, *Explanation in Geography*, Arnold, London (1969), pp. 470–80.
54. I. G. Heggie, Are gravity and interactance models a valid technique for planning regional transport facilities? *Operational Research Quarterly*, **20** (1969), pp. 93–110.
55. B. J. L. Berry, *Essays on Commodity Flows and the Spatial Structure of the Indian Economy*, University of Chicago, Department of Geography, Research Paper no. 111, Chicago (1966), pp. 189–237.
56. *Op. cit.*, p. 192.
57. *Op. cit.*, p. 238.
58. E. L. Ullman, The role of transportation and the bases for interaction, in W. L. Thomas (ed.), *Man's Role in Changing the Face of the Earth*, University of Chicago Press, Chicago (1956), pp. 862–80.
59. W. Bunge, *Theoretical Geography*, Lund Studies in Geography, series C, General and mathematical geography, no. 1 (second edition, 1966), p. 125.
60. *Op. cit.*, p. 867.

61. A. G. Wilson, *op. cit.*
62. R. H. T. Smith, Toward a measure of complementarity, *Economic Geography*, **40** (1964), pp. 1–8.
63. Stouffer, *op. cit.*
64. *Op. cit.*, p. 868.
65. Stouffer, *op. cit.*, p. 846.
66. Ullman, *op. cit.*, pp. 868–9.
67. M. E. Eliot Hurst, Land use/travel movement relationships, *Traffic Quarterly*, **23** (1969), pp. 263–74.
68. R. M. Zettel and R. R. Carll, *Summary Review of Major Metropolitan Area Transportation Studies in the US*, Institute of Transportation and Traffic Engineering, University of California, Berkeley (1962).

10. THE INTERMODAL ALLOCATION OF FLOWS

1. B. T. Bayliss and S. L. Edwards, *Transport for Industry*, HMSO, London (1968).
2. Traders Road Transport Association, *Survey of C-licensed Vehicles*, London (1959), and Aims of Industry, *Integration in Freight Transport*, London (1968).
3. Bayliss and Edwards, *op. cit.*, p. 39.
4. A. A. Walters, *Integration in Freight Transport*, Institute of Economic Affairs, Research Monograph 15, London (1968), p. 58.
5. *Ibid.*, pp. 60–1.
6. *Ibid.*, p. 59, and Bayliss and Edwards, *op. cit.*, p. 43.
7. Price alone is used as a determinant by E. D. Perle, *The Demand for Transportation*, University of Chicago, Department of Geography, Research Paper no. 95 (1964).
8. M. Beckmann, C. B. McGuire and C. B. Winsten, *Studies in the Economics of Transportation*, Yale U.P. for Cowles Commission, New Haven (1956), pp. 113–17.
9. A. G. Wilson, The use of entropy maximising models in the theory of trip distribution, mode split and route split, *Journal of Transport Economics and Policy*, **3** (1969), pp. 108–126.
10. F. R. Wilson, *Journey to Work*, Maclaren, London (1967).
11. R. Gronau, *The Value of Time in Passenger Transportation: the demand for air travel*, National Bureau for Economic Research, New York (1970).
12. M. J. Bruton, *Introduction to Transportation Planning*, Hutchinson, London (1970), chapter 6.
13. W. Adams, *Factors Influencing Mass Transit and Automobile Travel in Urban Areas*, as quoted by F. R. Wilson, *op. cit.*
14. D. S. Hill and H. C. van Cube, Development of a model forecasting travel mode choice in urban areas, *Highway Research Board Record*, no. 38 (1963).
15. F. R. Wilson, *op. cit.*, pp. 208–13.
16. A. G. Wilson, Interregional commodity flows: entropy maximising approaches, *Geographical Analysis*, **2** (1970), p. 282.

11 DECISION MAKING AND GOVERNMENT POLICY
   IN THE TRANSPORT SECTOR

1. P. D. Henderson, Notes on public investment criteria in the United Kingdom, *Bulletin of the Oxford University Institute of Economics and Statistics*, 27 (1965), pp 58–89.
2. D. Teichroew, A. A. Robichek and M. Montalbano, An analysis of criteria for investment and financing decisions under certainty, *Management Science*, 12 (1965), pp. 151–79.
3. C. D. Foster and M. E. Beesley, Estimating the social benefit of constructing an underground railway in London, *Journal of the Royal Statistical Society*, 126 (1963), pp. 46–58.
4. Henderson, *loc. cit.*
5. W. L. Garrison and M. E. Marts, *Geographic Impact of Highway Improvement*, University of Washington, Highway Economic Studies (1958), chapter 4.
6. Commission on the Third London Airport, *Report*, HMSO, London (1971), pp. 119–30.
7. Henderson, *op. cit.*
8. E. J. Mishan, A reappraisal of the principles of resource allocation, *Economica*, 24 (1957), p. 337.
9. H. C. Bos and L. M. Koyck, *The Appraisal of Investments in Transportation Projects: a practical example*, Netherland Economic Institute, Rotterdam (1958).
10. For a discussion of these categories see E. L. Ullman, Geographical prediction and theory, in S. B. Cohen, *Problems and Trends in American Geography*, Basic Books, New York (1967), pp. 124–45.
11. Ullman, *op. cit.*, *passim*.
12. Ministry of Transport, *Portbury: reasons for the Minister's decision not to authorise the construction of a new dock at Portbury, Bristol*, HMSO, London (1966), annex 4.
13. M. F. Tanner and A. F. Williams, Port development and national planning strategy, *Journal of Transport Economics and Policy*, 1 (1967), pp. 315–24.
14. M. E. Beesley, T. M. Coburn and D. J. Reynolds, *The London–Birmingham Motorway: traffic and economics*, Road Research Technical Paper no. 46, HMSO, London (1960), pp. 18–36 and 87.
15. Foster and Beesley, *op. cit.*
16. Ministry of Transport, *Rural Bus Services*, HMSO, London (1961), chapter 2.
17. *Ibid.*, paragraphs 17–20.
18. D. St J. Thomas, *The Rural Transport Problem*, Routledge and Kegan Paul, London (1963), chapters 5 and 9.
19. *Rural Bus Services in Denbighshire*, report of working party, Denbighshire County Council, Ruthin (1971), appendices A, B and C.
20. Thomas, *op. cit.*, pp. 65–70.
21. *Ibid.*, p. 65.

22. *Rural Bus Services*, chapter 7.
23. Ministry of Transport, *Rural Bus Services: report of local inquiries*, HMSO, London (1965), p. 7, Thomas, *op. cit.*, p. 165, *Rural Bus Services, op. cit.*, p. 33.
24. K. M. Gwilliam, *Transport and Public Policy*, Allen and Unwin, London (1964), part IV.
25. C. I. Savage, *An Economic History of Transport*, Hutchinson, London (1966), p. 172.
26. Gwilliam, *op. cit.*, p. 214.
27. M. R. Bonavia, *The Economics of Transport*, Cambridge University Press (1957 edition), chapter 6.
28. H. O. Mance, *The Road and Rail Transport Problem*, Pitman, London (1941).
29. E. J. Mishan, *The Costs of Economic Growth*, Penguin, Harmondsworth (1969), pp. 113–35.
30. *The Reshaping of British Railways, op. cit.*, pp. 40–1.
31. *Ibid.*, p. 41.
32. B. T. Bayliss, *European Transport*, Mason, London (1965), p. 101.
33. *Ibid.*, p. 111.
34. A. Hazlewood, *Rail and Road in East Africa*, Blackwell, Oxford (1964), chapter 6.
35. Ministry of Transport, *The Transport of Freight*, HMSO, London (1967).
36. A. A. Walters. *Integration in Freight Transport*, Institute of Economic Affairs, Research Monograph no. 15, London (1968), chapter 5.
37. Ministry of Transport, *Carriers' Licensing*, HMSO, London (1965). p. 74.
38. *Carriers' Licensing, op. cit.*, chapter 2.
39. *Ibid.*, p. 23.
40. As reported by Hazlewood, *op. cit.*, pp. 44–51.

Index